POOR RELIEF
in
DURHAM, LEE
and
MADBURY

New Hampshire

1732-1891

ഌരു

Timothy Dodge
B.A., Swarthmore College, 1979
M.L.S., Columbia University, 1980
M.A., University of New Hampshire, 1982
Ph.D., University of New Hampshire, 1992

Thesis
Submitted to the University of New Hampshire
in Partial Fulfillment of
the Requirement for the Degree of
Master of Arts in History
September, 1982

HERITAGE BOOKS
2012

HERITAGE BOOKS
AN IMPRINT OF HERITAGE BOOKS, INC.

Books, CDs, and more—Worldwide

For our listing of thousands of titles see our website
at
www.HeritageBooks.com

Published 2012 by
HERITAGE BOOKS, INC.
Publishing Division
100 Railroad Ave. #104
Westminster, Maryland 21157

Copyright © 1995 Timothy Dodge

All rights reserved. No part of this book may be reproduced or transmitted in any form or by any means, electronic or mechanical, including photocopying, recording or by any information storage and retrieval system without written permission from the author, except for the inclusion of brief quotations in a review.

International Standard Book Numbers
Paperbound: 978-0-7884-0150-3
Clothbound: 978-0-7884-9330-0

Table of Contents

Acknowledgements v

CHAPTER *PAGE*

I. Early American Poor Relief 1

II. "Outdoor" Relief to the 1830s 21

III. The Town Farm System 43

IV. Post-Civil War Poor Relief 67

V. Conclusion 87

Appendix 97

Bibliography 121

Acknowledgements

I would like to express my great appreciation here for the help and encouragement provided by Professor Robert Mennel, who directed my work in all its stages. Thanks are also due to Professors Robert Gilmore and Charles Clark, who were my readers. I would also like to thank William Copeley of the New Hampshire Historical Society Library for locating a number of obscure documents, as did the staffs of the Durham Museum, the Dover Public Library, the University of New Hampshire Library, and the Lee Town Library. Finally, my parents, Peter and Renata Dodge, deserve my gratitude for encouragement and helpful suggestions.

CHAPTER I

Early American Poor Relief

American methods of poor relief underwent several major modifications from the colonial days through the late nineteenth century. These changes were based on differing perceptions of the cause of poverty. From "outdoor" relief, in which paupers were boarded with private families or received aid in their own homes, the trend changed to "indoor" relief, which confined paupers to the town poor farm. The county poor farm eventually supplemented or replaced the town institution. This period of time also saw poor relief change from a local town concern to a matter administered on the county and state level. These changes were gradual, and some of the older forms of relief persisted alongside the newer developments.

Poor relief of the eighteenth and nineteenth centuries at the local level can be examined in three small towns in Strafford County, New Hampshire: Durham, Lee, and Madbury. Original records are extant, covering the period from the towns' incorporations in 1732, 1766, and 1768, respectively, onwards. These documents vary greatly in completeness. They consist mainly of financial information and records of town business. *Town of Durham Accounts 1751-1782* and *Town Book. Treasurer's Record 1755-1826* are very helpful in providing financial information on eighteenth century poor relief in Durham and Madbury. The *Lee Town Records 1766-1815* are almost useless in this respect, but they do describe methods of relief, persons involved, and so on. The typed transcript of the Durham *Town Records* for 1732-1841 has been one of the most valuable sources for this paper: hundreds of clearly legible pages. Many of the older sources consist of yellowed, faded, torn, and stained pages covered with handwriting which varies from fairly neat to virtually illegible. The *Lee Payment Books* and *Daybooks* covering the period 1802-1842 are a good example of this type of source.

All three towns have small collections of miscellaneous papers on the late eighteenth and early nineteenth centuries, which contain some very useful items. For example, the Madbury miscellaneous papers of 1768-1799 include several valuable handwritten contracts for town paupers "let out" to the lowest bidder. So also do the records for Durham.

One of the most useful sources of information for the period after 1840 is the printed town annual report. Not only are these reports easy on the reader's eyes, but they also have the desired information arranged neatly in one place. A disadvantage is their brevity. Occasionally they go into some depth on the question of town poor relief, but usually they are not as detailed as older town records and accounts of overseers of the poor. One useful source on the Lee poor farm is the handwritten inventory and appraisal which covers the years 1859-1873. Also helpful are the Lee town records (handwritten) for 1825-1851, 1862-1872, and 1872-1896, as well as those for Durham for the post-Civil War era. The printed annual reports of the Strafford County commissioners supply data on the county poor farm in Dover, for the years 1867-1891.

Through the following pages, poor relief practices in Durham, Lee, and Madbury will be investigated. We will cover "outdoor" relief of the eighteenth and early nineteenth centuries, the town poor farm system of the mid-nineteenth century ("indoor" relief), and the county poor farm system of the post-Civil War period. The degree to which local poor relief conformed to the national trends of poor relief will be considered here, as well as the effects of "indoor" relief.

Colonial Americans regarded their poor neighbors as an unfortunate, but natural, group in society. While generally sympathetic, attitudes ranged from pity to scorn. The main concern was for economy. If there was any way to avoid supporting a person from public funds, it was investigated.[1] A hardworking rural society had trouble enough supporting itself, especially in New England. Benjamin Franklin's gospel of industry, frugality, and sobriety was broadly applied here. The common belief was that if everyone followed such advice, no one need become destitute, and there would be little need for relief or charity.[2] At the heart of colonial poor relief was the distinction between the helpless poor such as cripples, widows, orphans, the elderly, and the insane, all of whom had some claim to aid, and the able-bodied "idlers and strangers" who were to be kept off public support. The "poor would be helped, but it must be proved that they could no longer help themselves and had no kin who owed them support."[3]

This seemingly ungenerous attitude and the distinction between deserving and undeserving paupers had its roots in sixteenth century England. Enormous economic and demographic changes in sixteenth century England created a displaced former peasantry who took to beggary and vagabondage to survive.[4] With beggars filling London's streets and with rural villages threatened by strolling vagabonds, old forms of charity were found to be inadequate. To meet this alarming development, Parliament passed the Poor Law of 1601, a measure which profoundly influenced early American efforts to deal with poverty. Public authorities made a distinction between able-bodied and infirm paupers, with the former being forced to labor for their own support in workhouses and the latter being maintained in almshouses. Administration of relief was a local affair conducted by the town. Old forms of charity, such as those practiced by the church, were continued too.

A crucial feature of this type of relief is that it was designed to relieve poverty rather than prevent it. Early American practice was the same.[5] Social attitudes of the seventeenth and eighteenth centuries helped confirm this approach. According to Samuel Mencher, poverty, like wealth, showed God's attitude toward an individual's efforts in this world.[6] Thus, able-bodied paupers were regarded with less sympathy than the infirm, but neither group was seen as unnatural.

Since most colonial Americans lived in isolated rural villages, poor relief was strictly a local affair. Province laws provided outlines to follow, but there was no centralization of relief. Hard economic conditions, coupled with a self-reliant attitude, made people very reluctant to take in poor strangers. Laws were made to keep nonresident paupers and other undesirable characters out of the community. A typical example is "An Act for Regulating Townships, Choice of Town Officers & Setting Forth Their Power," passed May 2, 1719, in New Hampshire. A three-month "warning out" period was established for nonresident paupers who came into town. If a person was not gone within fourteen days after his three-month grace period was over, the law directed that he be "conveyed from Constable to Constable into the Town where he properly belongs, or had his last residence at his own charge, if able to pay the same, or otherwise at the charge of the Town so sending him."[7]

As early as 1638, New Hampshire lawmakers recognized the right of towns to exclude strangers. Apparently some "warned out" persons were allowed to remain in town. But woe to such a person if he became indigent. Josiah Benton says that if a "warned out" person who resided in a town paid taxes, voted, or even held a town office, still the town was under no obligation at all to help him. Thus, according to Benton, "They might be taxed for the support of others who were in need, but when they came to be in need, they were entitled to no help from the taxes of the town."[8]

What was done in the case of paupers native to the town? In the largest towns such as Boston, the poor were generally taken care of via "indoor" relief. Infirm and old paupers were cared for in the almshouse, while the able-bodied labored in the workhouse picking oakum (used for caulking ships), weaving cloth, or making shoes.[9] Except for a few almshouses and workhouses present in the biggest settlements, most of the measures taken to relieve the poor were of a makeshift nature. "Outdoor" relief was practiced. Simply put, "outdoor" relief consisted of aid to paupers in a non-institutional setting (no almshouse). There were two main forms of "outdoor" relief: a) supplying the poor with aid in their own homes and b) boarding the poor in private homes.

The first form was applied to those either near dependency or too old or infirm to support themselves but still residing in their own homes. Most often this aid was in the form of supplies like firewood, clothing, and food. Cash was rarely disbursed. In Massachusetts, people near dependency were sometimes granted tax abatements.[10] Boarding the poor in private homes varied locally. For our purposes, the "New England method" is most relevant. The "New England method" was in essence an auction -- sometimes it was known as the "vendue," "bidding off," or "letting out the poor."[11] It worked as follows: usually once a year, the town paupers were assembled at a town meeting point or the house of a prominent citizen. There, like slaves at an auction, the paupers were set up for bids from the local townsmen gathered together. A pauper auction might even be a festive occasion with refreshments and entertainment.[12] However, there was one unusual feature about this kind of auction: the auctioneer (representing the town) was interested in making bids on the paupers as low as possible, because in this case the auctioneer paid out the final bid. For example, if one man bid $25 for a town pauper and another man bid $20, the man with the lower bid would receive the pauper into his house (usually for a year) and the town would pay him $20 to maintain this pauper. The $20 was to pay for the pauper's clothing, food, lodging, and so forth. Besides any monetary gain, the bidder would acquire a helping hand, since the pauper was expected to work for his bidder.

For later scholars of the subject, such as Benjamin J. Klebaner, this was the main evil of the "New England method" of poor relief. The townsmen assembled at a pauper auction were interested primarily in getting work from the pauper.[13] Sometimes the town paupers were auctioned off in lots to just one bidder. Started early in the eighteenth century, the vendue system flourished in the fifty or so years after the Revolutionary War. It was gradually abandoned in favor of other forms of relief, but lingered on in New Hampshire through the 1850s and later.[14]

A variation on the "New England method" was the practice of "binding out" poor children and orphans. Often, such a child was auctioned off like the adult paupers to the lowest bidder. At other times the child was "bound out" to local farmers, artisans, sea captains, or housewives for a certain time period. Written indentures in the form of contracts were signed to ensure fair play and to benefit the child. Also, Massachusetts passed a law in 1781 requiring that "bound out" children were taught to read and write.[15] Other states had similar provisions. Children were usually "bound out" until adulthood -- age eighteen for girls and twenty-one for boys.

"Binding out" reflected Franklin's utilitarian outlook. A system of education through apprenticeship was designed to solve the problems of idleness and pauperism by creating a supply of skilled workers.[16] "Binding out" also had a moral emphasis in colonial New Hampshire. A concurrent vote of the Council and Assembly in 1712 made provisions to combat "Ignorance, Ill Manners, and Irreligion" evident in poor children neglected by their parents or masters.[17]

In case of sickness, a dependent person could expect to receive one of two types of aid from the community: material aid or medical care. Depending on the ill person's condition, he might receive medical supplies, food, and firewood in his own home. In other cases, the town would pay a doctor to administer to the patient at home or at the home where he was being boarded. Sometimes the patients were boarded at the doctor's home at town expense for treatment.[18] Just as all the paupers in a given town might be "let out" to one person, so too, the medical care of all the town's poor might be delegated to one doctor.[19]

At times local resources for coping with poverty were strained by unusual circumstances. Indian wars, the French and Indian War, the Revolution, and the War of 1812 were such happenings. Women and children left behind by the men enlisted as soldiers were forced to seek public aid if their relatives were unable to support them. Sometimes the returning husband was too ill or injured to support his own family; thus adding still another burden to the public treasury.

Sometimes epidemics would throw people on relief. Fires could ruin a person overnight. In such cases when town funds were inadequate, the overseers of the poor might call on the local church for special collections for alms.[20]

Throughout the colonial period and until the 1820s, "outdoor" relief measures were prevalent. "Indoor" relief was extremely limited. According to David J. Rothman, the typical eighteenth century almshouse "looked and was run like an ordinary household" or posited no reform scheme different from "outdoor" relief systems.[21] Both were manifestations of a certain attitude as well as limited available resources. Since the poor were regarded as a natural phenomenon, there was no real alarm about their presence.

Until the rise of Andrew Jackson, American society displayed some degree of deferential relations. There was no aristocracy in the European sense, but there were prominent local squires and gentlemen whose wealth and family connections placed them in the position of community leaders. The existing social order was considered to be under God's approval; thus, poverty was normal and its relief was necessary and appropriate. The poor provided an opportunity for the rich to do good works.[22] Until the 1820s, then, poverty was not seen as anything abnormal. It was a condition which could be met on the local level.

Economic, demographic, and social changes in early nineteenth century America were to change this picture greatly. Starting around 1825, there was a national shift from "outdoor" methods of relief to "indoor" relief (the confinement of paupers to poor farms and other asylums). What was the reason for such a change?

First, population growth and massive expansion in territory changed the patterns of settlement. New and more efficient modes of transportation began to link the country together. While the rural village was still home for most Americans, the rate of urbanization began to exceed the general rate of population growth. Related to this denser and more connected population was the emergence of a new sense of American nationalism, particularly after the War of 1812. The prospect of ever more prosperity and territorial expansion contributed to this feeling.

By the 1820s Americans began to notice poverty in a new way. Slums in cities and significant numbers of poor immigrants made poverty a much more visible phenomenon. Early efforts at industrialization placed increasingly larger numbers of people at the mercy of economic trends. Upper- and middle-class Americans reacted with fear and distaste to the poor. Pity was disappearing and the poor were becoming "the dangerous classes."[23] The upper and middle classes wondered how poverty could exist in the land of plenty and opportunity. The increasingly common belief that individual effort alone accounted for one's condition meant that paupers were increasingly blamed for their condition.

Because of these massive economic and social changes, the old stable view of poverty became outmoded. Now the poor were seen as a social problem: they were draining the community's resources, demoralizing America's laborers, and they were a source of unrest.[24] The pauper, once viewed as an unfortunate, pitiful figure, was now becoming someone strange and even dangerous. Just as the horrible aspects of crime, insanity, and alcoholism were brought to the public's attention, so too, pauperism was becoming sensationalized.

Josiah Quincy's *Report of 1821 on the Pauper Laws of Massachusetts* was an early expression of the new concern with poverty. The influence of the old English Poor Law is still visible in Quincy's distinction between the "impotent" and "able" poor. For Quincy, the real problem was the latter type of paupers. Their existence encouraged "habits of idleness, dissipation and extravagance among the class which labor."[25] Methods of poor relief were examined in the *Report*. Quincy expressed the new uncharitable attitude when he concluded, "The just pride of independence so honorable to man in every condition is thus corrupted by the certainty of public provisions."[26] Previously, relief had been given in a charitable manner, or at worst, grudgingly. Still, the principle of relief had never been questioned much before. But, since some measures had to be taken, Quincy concluded that almshouses were better by far than "outdoor" relief. In almshouses the poor could be set to work and their morals could be supervised. If town poor received aid in their own homes they would become even lazier, and what was worse, indulge in alcohol. Quincy believed that intemperance was the most common cause of pauperism.[27] Quincy also reflected the common complaint of established groups that the stability and cohesion of the eighteenth century community had disappeared.

Thus, with the poor now viewed as a distinct and dangerous group in society, new ways to handle the problem of pauperism had to be found. The almshouse was seen as the answer. It was not a new method, so why was it seized upon so eagerly?

Primarily, it is important to emphasize the growth of reform as a general response to social change. In the period roughly between the 1820s and the Civil War, various reform movements flourished. Charitable societies were founded in a number of cities to help alcoholics, the insane, blacks and slaves, orphans, immigrants, and other unfortunates. Social and economic changes converged with various religious and philosophic developments to produce a "moral fundamentalism."[28] Reform movements were designed to harmonize man with the new moral order. Every institution in American society was criticized.[29] This included America's systems of poor relief. Since poverty was now perceived as a major new problem, the older methods of its relief were called into question. Reformers saw poverty as caused by the weakness of an individual's character or body; it was a curable condition. The solution was to build up a pauper's character rather than to just relieve his need.[30] Reformers had come up with a solution: the almshouse.

The almshouse became popular at the same time as the penitentiary and the insane asylum. Institutional confinement was the answer for many of society's ills. Reformers thought that the almshouse experience could actually rehabilitate the poor.[31] Following European examples, a specially designed program of work, education, and moral exhortation would do the trick, they thought. The problem could be taken care of by confining the paupers (or criminals or lunatics) within institutions where they would be rehabilitated and kept out of mischief. Under supervision, they would have no opportunity to lapse into vice, idleness, and intemperance. The New York Legislature's *Relief and Settlement of the Poor* (1824) expressed this reforming motive in vigorous language. While confined to the workhouse, "sturdy beggars and vagrants" were to submit to a regimen "either of confinement upon a rigid diet, hard labor, employment at the stepping mill, or some treatment equally efficacious in restraining their vicious appetites and pursuits."[32]

One should not assume that all almshouses were administered as vigorously as those recommended by the New York Legislature, even those in New York. Conditions varied greatly. The most radical programs were usually found in the cities, but some idealistic reformers also established a few model almshouses in the country.

In most places only the minimum effort was made.[33] This was especially true in rural areas where there was little money available. The almshouse in such places was usually just an old farm bought by the town for the use of the poor.[34] This was the start of the "town poor farm" system, which flourished in the northern half of the United States for most of the nineteenth century. In many cases, the farm, which was bought at the least cost to the town, was in poor condition. Repairs might be made and buildings attached to the central structure. Ideally, the poor would be set to various tasks by the farm superintendent; the farm was to keep the paupers usefully employed and possibly even pay for itself. But practice did not always follow principle.

By the 1840s the almshouse system was in full swing. In most areas of the United States, auctioning and boarding out of paupers was disappearing. So too was "outdoor" relief, in which the poor received cash and kind in their own homes.[35] Throughout the country there was an increasing reliance on the almshouse system. The conditions varied greatly from one almshouse to another. As time went on, many faults were found with the almshouse system. As early as the 1830s the almshouse was known as a "symbol of mismanagement, political chicanery and corruption, public apathy and wretchedness."[36] What went wrong?

For one thing, there was no real provision made for pauper classification. Almshouses were often used as deposits for all of society's outcasts and misfits, not just paupers. Kelso comments, "They housed little children with the prostitute, the vagrant, the drunkard, the idiot, and the maniac."[37]

Local authorities had seized upon the new method of poor relief, the almshouse, as the ultimate solution, with little thought of potential drawbacks. Paradoxically, the several decades preceding the Civil War did see new attention given to separate classes of the unfortunate. Orphanages spread rapidly. Reform schools for juvenile offenders appeared in the Midwest and Eastern cities. Institutions for the blind and deaf were started. Noteworthy efforts by reformers such as Dorothea Dix were made to alleviate the miserable conditions of the insane. But, for many towns, "pauperism" was a catch-all term that continued to encompass people of all ages and conditions.

Political chicanery also contributed to the failure of the almshouse system. Administration of the local poor house or farm could be "the cheapest of the spoils of politics for plunder only."[38] Reformers of the 1890s railed against this phenomenon, which had its start in the 1830s. In political contests there were a number of prizes to be won, and sometimes the administration of poor relief was one of them. Thanks to the spoils system ethos of Andrew Jackson's day, nearly everywhere someone on the winning political side might expect to be appointed superintendent of the almshouse or overseer of the poor, or to be put in charge of poor relief funds. Budgets could be diverted so that some of this money went into the pockets of the appropriate official; paupers suffered because of this. Many almshouses became drafty, dirty, and rundown places. Food was coarse.

Because little or no provision was made for the differing conditions of paupers, treatment tended to be uniform. Usually no distinctions were made between able-bodied and infirm paupers, which meant that almshouses became depositories for all unfortunate and undesirable persons. Rather than waste their time cooped up with the aged, idiotic, crippled, lazy, drunk, and wretched inmates of the town almshouse, able-bodied paupers tended to avoid incarceration in such an institution.[39] Sadly enough, the public was generally unaware of and indifferent to the deterioration of the almshouse. The problem of "sturdy beggars and vagrants" was not solved. Many took to the road, causing social critics of a later time to decry the presence of so many tramps in America.

The almshouse system also failed because administrative procedures tended to become fossilized over time. When the original reforming impetus died down, the local community continued to rely on the principles laid down in the 1820s and '30s. A number of almshouses were established simply because they were the latest trend. By the 1850s, when the faults of the almshouse system were becoming noticeable, it was too late to change. Bureaucratic procedures had been established, and new methods of poor relief were not yet in sight. It was too cumbersome to revive old methods of relief, which would have seemed reactionary in any case. People were less inclined to keeping the poor in their own homes.

However, the old methods were not completely dead even by the 1850s.[40] Rural villages were slow to catch on to the almshouse trend. Resources were not always adequate to meet the expense of purchasing a town farm. In many instances there was a combination of old and new methods. A town farm might be in operation and at the same time some forms of "outdoor" relief would also be relied on.

By the 1850s, the town almshouse or poor farm was increasingly portrayed as a failure. A typical description relied on sensational details to shock the reader: "Here was an insane woman raving and uttering wild gibberings; a half crazy man was sardonically grinning; and an overgrown idiotic boy was torturing one of the little boys, while securely holding him, by thrusting splinters under his fingernails."[41] The prevalence of similar accounts indicates that such conditions existed in many nineteenth century almshouses.

While the almshouse system was spreading throughout the land, the problem of poverty was receiving national attention for the first time. Starting in 1850, and proceeding through 1890, the United States government compiled statistics on pauperism. The first national description of the problem is in the *Statistical View of the United States* by J.D.B. DeBow, Superintendent of the United States Census. Table CLXXIII, "Pauperism in the United States, 1850," provides very basic figures on the number of paupers and the annual cost of poor relief for each state.[42] With each new census, the statistics on pauperism became more sophisticated and detailed. By 1880 one finds Table CXIII, "The Defective, Dependent, and Delinquent Classes: The Almshouse Paupers of the United States in 1880." In this table, the "form of disability" was tabulated under fourteen headings ranging from "Destitute" to "Lame and Crippled" to "Old Age."[43]

As poverty came to be perceived as a national problem, local resources and methods of poor relief were seen to be inadequate. Two developments occurred: a) the centralization of poor relief administration into county and state units and b) the rise of state boards of charities and corrections, and private charities with a renewed emphasis on reform.

The increased involvement of county and state governments in poor relief sprang in part from the large increase in mobile paupers. Their appearance was due to huge population increases, immigration, and improvements in transportation. Massive social and economic disruptions caused by the Civil War also contributed, as did economic crises in 1857-1858, 1873-1879, and 1893-1897. Even more than in the past, towns took measures to exclude tramps and other people likely to become public charges.

The New Hampshire laws reveal a great concern with the settlement of paupers. Following a detailed list of residence qualifications, Chapter 81, "Settlement of Paupers," of Title 10, New Hampshire Laws, says, "No person shall have a home for the purpose of gaining a settlement while assisted as a pauper."[44] The first explicit distinction between "town" and "county" paupers in New Hampshire was made in the *Revised Statutes of the State of New Hampshire: Passed December 23, 1842*. There had been some previous provisions for reimbursing towns for supporting nonresident paupers, but they had been complicated and for exceptional cases only. The law of 1842 declared that within one year of the relief or burial of a nonresident pauper, the town overseer of the poor might present an account of funds expended on the pauper to the county treasurer, who was to repay the town.[45]

In other states, too, the fear of becoming saddled with the expense of nonresident paupers prompted the passage of similar laws. By the time of the Civil War, a new institution was appearing in America: the almshouse. The county almshouse received both town paupers and paupers who had no settlement. Massachusetts went further in centralizing relief administration. As early as 1854 there were state poor farms to deal with nonresident paupers. Located at Tewksbury, Bridgewater, and Monson, they had a capacity of five hundred each.[46]

Massachusetts also created the first central state supervisory authority in America.[47] This was the Massachusetts Board of State Charities, founded in 1863. It consisted of five members appointed by the governor with the advice and consent of the council. The members had staggered terms in office. The Board was essentially a supervisory organization which made reports on the state, county, and local institutions. It also had the power to transfer paupers from one institution to another.[48] Other states were slow to follow Massachusetts. State boards of charities established after Massachusetts were Ohio and New York in 1867; Illinois, North Carolina, Pennsylvania, and Rhode Island in 1869; Wisconsin and Michigan in 1871; and Kansas and Connecticut in 1873. New Hampshire did not have a state board until the mid 1890s. Thus, centralization of relief administration was a gradual and uneven process. Some areas combined the relief of paupers with that of all other types of relief. In others there were separate departments for the poor, orphans, criminals, handicapped, and others.

Closely related to the phenomenon of centralized relief was the rise in private charity organizations throughout America. Immigration from the country and from Europe was packing the cities to an unprecedented degree. If anything, poverty was even more visible and appalling in the late 1800s than in the 1820s, when it first received widespread attention among established groups. Charities played an important role in defining social action, in response to the depressions of 1873-1879 and 1893-1897. They also criticized sharply the almshouse system as encouraging dependency. They approached poverty in a new way: data were collected from industrial employment figures, the police, tenement house inspectors, settlement houses, trade union statistics, and neighborhood surveys.[49] The significance of these observations was that they provided the basis for a new interpretation of poverty in the late nineteenth century.

The major innovation of this new perspective was the distinction made between those paupers who were held responsible for their condition and those whose poverty was caused by forces out of their control. This went beyond the old distinction between able-bodied and infirm paupers. Now there was increasing recognition that vast impersonal forces, such as economic depressions, could be responsible for a pauper's condition.[50] Much publicity was given to the ill effects that life in the slums had on children. Perhaps the most influential book on this subject was *How the Other Half Lives* by Jacob Riis (1890).

An environmental interpretation was applied by reformers to a critique of existing methods of poor relief. That old whipping boy, the almshouse, was blamed by Homer Folks in 1894 for contributing to the problem of poverty. "It is a simple statement of fact that the majority of children who grow to adolescence in poorhouses become paupers or criminals." Proclaiming the new gospel, Folks continues, "Do we realize even yet to how great an extent every human being is the natural product of his surroundings?" He even asserts that there is such a thing as a poorhouse child type: "lazy, profane, cunning, immoral, absolutely untruthful, quarrelsome, and bold."[51]

However, as was true with earlier perceptions of poverty, there were still differing interpretations and opinions heldover from the past. A contrast to Folks' environmental interpretation is the uncharitable view expressed by A.O. Wright in 1889: "There are three things in which an average pauper delights -- dirt, disorder, and idleness." The ancient distrust of the able-bodied poor is evident too: "The labor test is the best practical test that has ever been devised to sift out the really needy, and therefore deserving, from those who can, but will not, earn their own living."[52] The old bugbear of intemperance was once more cited by reformers as a cause of poverty.

The diversity of attitudes toward poverty was met by a diversity of methods used to combat it. By the 1890s there were essentially three levels of poor relief practiced in the United States: 1) local "outdoor" relief via disbursements of money or supplies and local "indoor" relief via the almshouse on the town or county level; 2) local charities; and 3) state control via state institutions or state boards of charities. By and large, the almshouse was an impersonal institution used as a convenient depository for paupers. County and state efforts at least tried to impose minimum standards. They helped deal with nonresident paupers. State institutions for special cases such as blind or insane paupers helped relieve some of the misery in the local almshouse. State supervision of local institutions was practiced, at varying degrees.

Additionally, numerous private charities flourished at the end of the nineteenth century. The Charity Organization Societies (founded in London in 1869) encouraged better administration of these private charitable efforts. Essentially, the goal of the C.O.S. was to supervise private charities so that money would not be wasted on those paupers whom the organizations deemed unworthy.[53] Blanche D. Coll goes so far as to say, "To the C.O.S. all relief was at best a necessary evil."[54] Private charities made real attempts to differentiate among the poor by visiting individual poor families in their own homes. However, the charities usually had limited funds for operation and inadequate staffs to do the job.[55] Very few of these charities operated in rural areas. Nationally, private charities were at their peak in involvement in poor relief during the period from 1890 to 1914.[56] The trend after this period was toward gradual centralization of relief administration and other improvements; and this led into the development of public welfare, which was introduced by the New Deal in the 1930s.

Thus, a conventional summary of American poor relief between the colonial period and the late nineteenth century would indicate several changes. At first, "outdoor" relief dominated.

Paupers were aided in a non-institutional setting by local citizens or officials. In only a few cities was "indoor" relief practiced, by placing the poor in an almshouse. Attitudes toward the poor at this time ranged from sympathetic to hostile, but there was an acceptance of poverty as a natural condition in society.

Starting in the 1820s, poverty was regarded as an alarming new phenomenon. Economic and demographic changes were mainly responsible for its new visibility. In many cases the poor themselves were blamed for their condition. Reformers of the time regarded institutional confinement as the best remedy. Supposedly the concentration of the poor in one place and their subjection to a routine of work would convert them from a useless and dangerous class of people to worthy citizens. "Indoor" relief was widely applied in the 1830s and '40s. Thanks to mismanagement, corruption, apathy, and ignorance, the almshouse system was by and large a failure. Paupers were not rehabilitated. Almshouses became notorious as deposits for town misfits and undesirables.

From the mid-nineteenth century on, the administration of poor relief was gradually centralized. From being exclusively a town affair, the county and then the state governments began to assume a role in handling poor relief. County almshouses were established, often in response to the growing number of vagrants. Some state institutions were formed, mainly to deal with special groups like the blind, the insane, or children. The influence of reformers sometimes prompted the formation of state supervisory boards to regulate and inspect local and county institutions.

Toward the end of the nineteenth century, charitable organizations began to assume a prominent public position. They criticized existing relief institutions. They engaged in "outdoor" relief by making charitable visits to poor families in their own homes. An important related development was the realization of some reformers that at least some paupers were not responsible for their lot. External factors such as the slum or almshouse environment were examined, as well as the effects of economic depressions.

Historians differ in their assessment of the various relief measures taken. Nearly all agree that in practice the almshouse was a failure. The important disagreement is over the *principle* of "indoor" relief. Alice F. Tyler takes a fairly favorable view of the almshouse in *Freedom's Ferment*. She sees the almshouse as a progressive measure; in fact, she calls it a "valiant" effort.[57] In his *Poor Law to Poverty Program*, Samuel Mencher criticizes the almshouse as a demoralizing institution, but nevertheless considers it to be superior to the old "outdoor" forms of relief.

Holding another opinion, David J. Rothman regards the introduction of the almshouse as a baneful occurrence. *The Discovery of the Asylum* is a study of the failure of the almshouse, insane asylum, and penitentiary. Rothman's work is a good example of the new social history approach. His basic assumption is that a society can be best understood in terms of its institutional forms and arrangements.[58]

Barbara G. Rosenkrantz criticizes Rothman's revisionist position. She notes that his view of the institutions devised to handle poor people and others in nineteenth century America is conspiratorial; *i.e.*, the planned social control efforts of local elites. Rosenkrantz further notes that Rothman fails to distinguish between the intent behind the almshouse and its consequences because his overall anti-institutional bias is so strong.[59]

Local poor relief efforts of the eighteenth and nineteenth centuries can be examined in the three small towns of Durham, Lee, and Madbury in Strafford County, New Hampshire. This study has been extended to 1891 to cover the developments in poor relief described in the secondary sources: "outdoor" relief, the town poor farm system, and the county poor farm system.

Two main considerations will be kept in mind here. The first is the degree to which poor relief in Durham, Lee, and Madbury conformed to the national trends described so far. The second is whether an optimistic or pessimistic assessment of the almshouse applies here.

NOTES TO CHAPTER I

1. Samuel Mencher, *Poor Law to Poverty Program* (Pittsburgh, Pa., 1967), 45.

2. Robert H. Bremner, *American Philanthropy* (Chicago, 1960), 16.

3. Robert W. Kelso, *The History of Public Poor Relief in Massachusetts 1620-1920* (Boston, 1922), 33.

4. *Ibid.*, 17.

5. Merle Curti, "American Philanthropy and the National Character," *American Quarterly*, 10 (1958), 421.

6. Mencher, *Poor Law to Poverty Program*, 43.

7. Albert S. Batchellor, ed., *Laws of New Hampshire*, 2 (Concord, N.H., 1913), 344.

8. Josiah H. Benton, *Warning Out in New England* (Boston, 1911), 116.

9. Gary B. Nash, *The Urban Crucible* (Cambridge, Mass., 1979), 126.

10. Kelso, *Poor Relief in Massachusetts*, 103.

11. Benjamin J. Klebaner, "Pauper Auctions: The 'New England Method' of Poor Relief," *Essex Institute Historical Collections*, 91 (1955), 195.

12. *Ibid.*, 195.

13. *Ibid.*, 199.

14. *Ibid.*, 204.

15. Robert H. Bremner, *Children and Youth in America*, I (Cambridge, Mass., 1970), 266.

16. Marcus W. Jernegan, *Laboring and Dependent Classes in Colonial America 1607-1783* (New York, 1965), 101.

17. *Ibid.*, 111.

18. Albert Deutsch, "The Sick Poor in Colonial Times," *American Historical Review*, 46 (1941), 567.

19. *Ibid.*, 577.

20. Bremner, *American Philanthropy*, 25.

21. David J. Rothman, *The Discovery of the Asylum* (Boston, 1971), 42.

22. *Ibid.*, 17.

23. Robert H. Bremner, *From the Depths* (New York, 1956), 6.

24. Rothman, *Discovery of Asylum*, 155-156.

25. Cited in Sophonisba P. Breckinridge, *Public Welfare Administration in the United States*, 2nd. ed., (Chicago, 1938), 32.

26. *Ibid.*, 34.

27. *Ibid.*, 37.

28. Henry S. Commager, *The Era of Reform, 1830-1860* (New York, 1960), 7.

29. *Ibid.*, 10.

30. Bremner, *American Philanthropy*, 100-101.

31. Rothman, *Discovery of Asylum*, 180.

32. Cited in Breckinridge, *Public Welfare Administration*, 50.

33. Alice F. Tyler, *Freedom's Ferment* (Freeport, N.Y., 1970), 293.

34. Rothman, *Discovery of Asylum*, 196.

35. James Leiby, *Charity and Corrections in New Jersey* (New Brunswick, N.J., 1967), 18.

36. Bremner, *Children and Youth*, 631.

37. Kelso, *Poor Relief in Massachusetts*, 112.

38. Homer Folks, "The Removal of Children from Almshouses," *Proceedings of the National Conference of Charities and Correction*, (1894), 120.

39. Rothman, *Discovery of Asylum*, 239.

40. Kelso, *Poor Relief in Massachusetts*, 112.

41. William P. Letchworth, "The Removal of Children from Almshouses in the State of New York," *Proceedings of the National Conference of Charities and Correction* (1894), 133.

42. J.D.B. DeBow, *Statistical View of the United States* (Washington, 1854), 163.

43. Frederick H. Wines, *Report on the Defective, Dependent, and Delinquent Classes of the Population of the United States, As Returned at the Tenth Census (June 1, 1880)* (Washington, 1888) 465.

44. *The General Laws of New Hampshire* (Manchester, N.H., 1878), 197.

45. *The Revised Statutes of the State of New Hampshire; Passed December 23, 1842* (Concord, N.H., 1843), 139.

46. Kelso, *Poor Relief in Massachusetts*, 237.

47. Breckinridge, *Public Welfare Administration*, 237.

48. *Ibid.*, 248.

49. Leah H. Feder, *Unemployment Relief in Periods of Depression* (New York, 1936), 332.

50. *Ibid.*, 328.

51. Folks, "Removal of Children," *Proceedings*, (1894), 122-123.

52. A.O. Wright, "Employment in Poorhouses," *Proceedings of the National Conference of Charities and Correction*, (1889), 197 and 199.

53. Bremner, *From the Depths*, 51.

54. Blanche D. Coll, *Perspectives in Public Welfare: A History* (Washington, 1969), 44.

55. Rothman, *Discovery of Asylum*, 294.

56. Mencher, *Poor Law to Poverty Program*, 288.

57. Tyler, *Freedom's Ferment*, 294.

58. George H. Daniels, "Book Reviews," *Journal of American History*, 58 (March, 1972), 1016.

59. Barbara G. Rosenkrantz, "Booby-Hatch or Booby Trap: A New Look at Nineteenth Century Reform," *Social Research*, 39 (1972), 734-736.

CHAPTER II

"Outdoor" Relief To The 1830s

The towns of Durham, Lee, and Madbury had originally been part of Dover, where settlement began on Dover Point in 1623. In the eighteenth century Dover was partitioned into several new towns because of a growing diversity of economic and political interests and a feeling for local identity. Durham was separated from Dover in 1732, and it in turn was obliged to partition a portion of itself off to create Lee in 1766. Madbury already had a separate parish administration from that of Dover, since 1755. The "hiving" process, a common phenomenon in colonial New England, was completed in 1768 when Madbury became a town in its own right.

There are no reliable population figures for these towns until 1790. In that year Durham had 1247 inhabitants, Lee had 1029, and Madbury 592.[1] New Hampshire's entire population for 1790 consisted of 141,885 people. The five largest cities were Portsmouth with 4720 inhabitants, Rochester with 2852, Gilmantown with 2610, Londonderry with 2604, and Barrington with 2481. Stark's Location was the smallest in the state with only three inhabitants. Most towns had between five hundred and one thousand people.[2] Thus, Durham and Lee seem to have been good-sized towns and Madbury a fairly small one.

Government was very much a local matter in the eighteenth century. Aside from tax, military, and voting obligations to the province government, most governmental responsibilities devolved on the town. The official guidelines in the province laws illustrate the assumption that poor relief was a town matter: every New Hampshire town was supposed to elect one or more overseers of the poor.[3] In many cases, the overseers were also the town selectmen. Overseers were charged with estimating the amount of money needed to take care of the poor and supervising expenditures authorized by selectmen. The amount authorized was added to the rest of the tax rate, which was collected by the town constable.[4]

The localistic nature of poor relief and the fundamental definition of poverty were rooted in Elizabethan poor law. New Hampshire *Orders in Council* Chapter 39, dated November 30, 1687, simply declares that officials "provide for the necessary releife and maintainance of the Poore in each Towne in such Manner as by the Laws and Statutes of England."[5] This law made the local town government responsible for relief administration and encouraged distinctions in kind.

The issue was foremost in the minds of colonial New Englanders; poor relief was one of the very first items considered in the new town of Lee in 1766. The incorporating act declares that Lee's citizens "are chargeable with the Duty of Maintaining their Proportion and Part of such Poor as are now supported by the whole Town [of Durham]."[6] Even before Lee was partitioned off from Durham, town officials were planning the division of its burden. In 1764 a committee of the selectmen was chosen to make sure that the parish of Lee would "take their proportionable part of the poor." Again in the Durham town meeting of 1766, this measure was voted on and approved.[7]

The primacy of the town in poor relief was asserted when the Quakers of Lee put forth a proposal in 1768 that they be cleared from supporting any Lee paupers except those who were Quaker. The town voted negatively. Quakers and other religious groups did occasionally maintain their own paupers in other communities.[8]

"Outdoor" relief, "warning out," and almshouses were discussed in Chapter I. Let us examine the poor relief practices of Durham, Lee, and Madbury.

There were three possibilities: 1) the "New England method," otherwise known as "letting out" or "bidding off" the poor, and its variation known as "binding out" poor children; 2) "outdoor" relief with supplies or money provided to the pauper in his own residence; and 3) the almshouse. The almshouse may be discounted until the 1830s. Except for a proposal in Durham in 1762, which was defeated, there is no mention of almshouses in the three towns until the 1830s.[9] This leaves the first and second possibilities, which are amply documented in the records.

Poor Relief In Durham, Lee, and Madbury

Written indentures are extant for children "bound out" in Durham, Lee, and Madbury. Marcus Jernegan points out that there were three classes of children covered by such indentures: 1) apprentices, 2) children "put out" ("bound out") to service for their support by selectmen or overseers of the poor, and 3) children of illiterate parents or parents too poor to pay for their education.[10]

"An Act for Regulating Townships, Choice of Town Officers & Setting Forth Their Power" was passed May 2, 1719. This law declared, in the standard language of indentures, that selectmen or the overseers of the poor were to "Bind any poor children belonging to Such Town to be Apprenticed where they Shall see convenient, A Man Child until he Shall come to the age of Twenty one years, and a Woman Child until She Shall come to the age of Eighteen years or time of Marriage."[11]

The existence of several detailed indentures from the 1730s and '40s reveals that the "binding out" of poor children was practiced in Durham. The first indenture, dated March 26, 1729 (while Durham was still a part of Dover), concerned a boy named Richard White who was "bound out" to Jonathan Drew, a joiner. White's father was dead. The term was for twelve years and four months. The agreement is very detailed, a true contract with reciprocal obligations clearly stated. Young Richard was to "faithfully serve" Mr. and Mistress Drew, "keep their law," "gladly everywhere obey," and "do no damage to his said master or mistress." Other prohibitions included specify that "at any unlawful game he shall not play whereby his sd master or mistres [sic] may be damnified" and "he shall not absent himself by day nor night...without their consent."[12] In his turn, Jonathan the joiner was to "teach or cause him to be taught to read and write a legible hand and to syphor as far as reduction and to teach sd apprentis the art and trade of a joyner and to give him two good new suits of apparele...when his time is out and to provide for him meat, drink, washing, and lodging fit for an apprentice."[13] Besides Drew, two justices of the peace and all three town selectmen signed this contract. In the case of Richard White, it was the fact that the boy's father was dead which made it imperative that he be "bound out." Poverty was cited as George Barnes' reason for being "bound out" in 1747 to the cordwainer Joseph Sias: "Whereas Captain Barnes hath a son whose name is Geo. Barnes and being pore and not able to support him."[14]

Local records reveal few other indentures as detailed as those for Richard White and George Barnes. References to indentures are made in the records of Durham, Lee, and Madbury throughout the eighteenth and early nineteenth centuries. These show that "binding out" was applicable to a variety of paupers who were generally young.

In Madbury a "Negro Girl Named Nancy Being free Born in Said Parish and She Being Destitute of Father or Mother or any Other Relations to Help Her" was apprenticed to Patience Hill for a nine-year period starting on April 8, 1768.[15] A very young child named Aaron Davis was "bound out" to Jonathan Dockum of Lee for $16.00 in April, 1809. The boy, "aged between 4 and 5 years," was to receive six months' worth of schooling by age fourteen and another six months' worth by age twenty-one.[16] Finally, two indentures from Lee dated September 20, 1814, fit the typical description of "binding out" exactly. Abigail Hart was "bound out" to Abigail Wiggins until age eighteen ("if she shall arrive to that age"). She was to receive twenty months of schooling and two "good suits of cloths one new and the other partly worn." Mark Elliot was "bound out" to Lemuel Chesley for $14.50 until age twenty-one ("if he shall arrive to that time"). He was to receive two years of schooling and two suits.[17]

An unusual indenture concerning James Critchet of Durham was made in April, 1806. Instead of being "bound out" as a child until age twenty-one, Critchet was "bound out" for only one year to Thomas Jones. Critchet was no child, but a "single man upwards of forty years of age able to labour who has no visible means of support and lives idly persuing no lawful bisiness [sic]."[18] In many ways this resembles "letting out" the town poor to the lowest bidder (which will be discussed shortly), but the conditions are slightly different, and this indenture specifically states that Critchet is "put and bound out."

To summarize, children, especially orphans or homeless youths, were the objects of special concern. By "binding them out" the community prevented the appearance of young beggars, while the townsmen who took these children into their homes received cheap labor. It is impossible to tell from the available sources whether "binding out" was in practice a cruel or benevolent method. The detailed indentures of George Barnes and Richard White of Durham indicate that good behavior and strict obedience were expected of the children.

"Binding out" took care of pauper children. What was done for adult paupers? There were several ways to deal with these unfortunates. Because it resembles the "binding out" of poor children, the "letting out" system will be discussed first.

According to Benjamin J. Klebaner, the "New England method" of pauper auctions started early in the eighteenth century and flourished in the half-century following the American Revolution.[19] The records for Durham, Lee, and Madbury confirm the prevalence of the "New England method" of pauper auctions although none of the New Hampshire laws ever describe "letting out" the poor. "Letting out" was a local development; perhaps a local interpretation of the laws which stated only that overseers of the poor were to set paupers to work. However, as far back as the seventeenth century there were laws concerning work houses, which are based on the philosophy of the English Poor Law, and there is no reason to be surprised that the same philosophy might animate a less formal system. The animus shown toward able-bodied paupers is expressed in the title of a New Hampshire law from 1718: "An Act for Suppressing and Punishing of Rogues, Vagabonds, Common Beggars and Other Lewd, Idle, and Disorderly Persons, and Also for Setting the Poor to Work."[20] An act of 1766 is probably the closest thing to the "New England method" of poor relief. It gives the overseers of the poor power to set to work "all Such Persons tho of full age, Married or unmarried, of whatever Age they may be if able of Body to work, or perform the Service to be so appointed them."[21]

There was no set "bid" price. The amount of money a person received in exchange for boarding paupers varied quite widely. Factors such as health and age made a difference. Many poor children were "let out" like adults, rather than being "bound out." In most cases the town paid significantly smaller sums to those boarding these children than to those boarding adults.

This manner of poor relief suited Durham and Lee until the appearance of their town poor farms in the 1830s. Unfortunately there is a gap in Madbury's records between 1827 and 1852, which was the period during which the almshouse system took hold in America. However, the records for Madbury do indicate that the "binding out" of children and the "letting out" of adults was continued through at least 1827.

In 1751 William Willee of Durham was paid £2 5s for "supporting" Salathiel Denbo. Derry Pitman received £6 15s for "maintaining" Peter Denmore.[22] According to the available documents, Denbo and Denmore appear to have been the first Durham paupers maintained by the "letting out" system. The actual term "letting out the poor" does not appear in the records until 1754. However, Salathiel Denbo, Peter Denmore, and three other paupers are listed as being "supported" or "kept" in 1751.

In Lee there was debate on finding "Some method for the maintaining of phebe Randel" in 1769. An unspecified amount of money was raised for the "maintaining of Deliverance footman" too.[23] It is impossible to say whether these women were "let out" or not. The first definite account of the "letting out" system in Lee can be found in a tiny handwritten pamphlet entitled *Memorandum Book for 1784 and 1785*. Town paupers were "bid off" at the home of Captain Joseph Smith on April 14, 1784, and December 6, 1785. In 1784 Temperance Leathers was "Bidd off" to Clement Davis for £4 7s, Spencer Allen and his wife Ann were "Bidd off" to Thomas Tuttle for £21 12s, and Elizabeth Thompson went to Josiah Bartlett for £4 10s.[24] These are the first Lee paupers "bid off" on record.

Madbury became a separate parish from Dover in 1755, although it was not incorporated as a town until 1768. As a separate parish, Madbury was responsible for its own paupers. Thus, in 1756 we find that Timothy Perkins received £53 10s for "keeping" Edward Evens. Immediately following this in the *Treasurer's Record* is an entry for £3 spent "when Let out Edward Evens."[25]

For all three towns, the paupers listed as "bid off," "let out," or "put out" become more frequent after the 1780s. Like the "binding out" of children, "letting out" was a contract. All three towns have records of the conditions. An example is a document from Madbury dated April 18, 1786. It states:

> "To be Lett out this Day by the Selectmen of Madbury the Poor of said Madbury that wants relief the Conditions to be as follows [*viz*] for those Let out for one year only the parrish is to find Cloaths and they that takes any of said Poor is to find them Victuals Lodging & Washing Suitable for persons of their Capasity and if any Person or Persons shall agree to Take any of Said Poor by biding them off at a Vendue or Otherways and do not Comply with the a bove Conditions or the Conditions that may be then made for any of said Poor that may be Let out for any Longer time Shall pay the Cost of this Letting out of sid Poor and Six Shillings for Damages."[26]

Other such agreements explain the terms of the town's payment. In Madbury, those who bid for a pauper would be paid by offsetting their town taxes. If the bid turned out to be larger than this amount, the bidder received farm produce to make up the difference.[27] Durham residents supporting a pauper in 1798 were to receive payment by "orders on the collector of taxes."[28] As time went on, these contracts became more sophisticated. Thus, in Lee's conditions for "letting out" the poor in 1802, it was specified that payment was to be made in two installments at six-month intervals. In addition, clothing and medical bills were to be paid for separately by the town. Here, for the first time, the original sources mentioned that the poor were to be let out "to the lowest bid or bider, if the person be thought sufficient by the Selectmen."[29]

In exchange for assuming care of one or more paupers for (usually) the coming year, the bidder was paid by the town. The pauper's labor was also considered to be part of the bargain. For example, the "letting out" conditions for Madbury on April 12, 1793, specifically state, "the Person or Persons that takes any of the said Poor Are to have the Benifit of their Labour."[30]

Both parties were expected to abide by the conditions and, as noted, fines were levied for failure to comply with them. On March 22, 1802, Dr. William Guy of Lee was fined $2.00 "as forfeit for biding off Mary Muncy & not abiding the bid."[31] Shadrach Ham of Madbury forfeited $2.50 in 1795 "for not Supporting Susanner Evans according to agreement."[32]

Old and sick paupers were often boarded at a high cost to the town. For instance, Theodore Willey of Durham was paid £114 7s 6d for "Nussing Cloathing & Burying" Widow Drisco in 1764. At the same time, Deacon Stevens was paid only £26 12s 6d for "keeping" Lydia Boarman.[33] Similar examples abound in the records of Lee and Madbury. Sometimes a poor child was "bid off" to a townsman for nothing. Lee's "letting out" records for 1818 list twelve-year-old William Rollins as "bid off" to Reuben Bartlett "for nothing." His sister Sarah was also "bid off for nothing" to Benjamin Durgin. In contrast, the rest of the Lee paupers in 1818 were "bid off" at anywhere from $16.00 to $29.75.[34] No doubt Mr. Bartlett and Mr. Durgin counted on lots of work from the children and little in the way of maintenance costs.

Sometimes the standard "letting out" practice was modified. Weekly rather than annual charges might be made, or all of the town paupers might be "bid off" to one person. Weekly rates seem to have been charged for boarding children more than any other type of pauper. Durham tried the weekly rate on a large scale between 1799 and 1806, when nearly every pauper "let out" was maintained at a weekly charge.[35] In Lee in 1816, Daniel Runnels, a poor child, was "bid off" to Benjamin B. Tuttle for 50 cents a week. His brother George Runnels went to Mr. Tuttle for 75 cents a week.[36] If anything, this was more expensive than usual and much more expensive than "binding out." Perhaps the poor maintained at weekly rates were in a temporary position. In other words, until they were finally "let out" or "bound out" for a definite set period, someone had to maintain them. Since this temporary status was of unknown duration, a weekly charge seemed safest.

"Binding" and "letting out" for a year was by far the most common practice in Durham, Lee, and Madbury. Ezekial Twombly proposed to support all of the poor of Durham for one year in 1819. The selectmen agreed and Twombly was paid $995 to do so.[37] Twombly set a precedent for Durham. Competition to maintain all the town poor took place. The poor bill dropped lower when William Stilson "bid off" all the poor in 1820. Until the appearance of the town poor farm in 1834, the poor of Durham were "bid off" all in one lot to one man. From Twombly's charge of $995 in 1819, the bill dropped to $428 in 1826 when Jonathan Edgerley made his bid.[38] This practice does not seem to have been adopted in Madbury. In Lee, it is hard to determine. Starting in 1822, that town's records contain ambiguous entries, such as Daniel York receiving $120 "for taking care of poor" and Paul Giles receiving $150 "for keeping the poor."[39] This type of entry is uncommon, and in the mid-1820s the records revert back to the usual itemized listings of expenses for individual pauper maintenance.

Several cases exemplify the difficulty of calculating the expenses of poor relief. One example is the case of Salathiel Denbo of Durham. From 1751 through 1761 he was maintained as a town pauper. The following entries for 1751 indicate how difficult it is to separate the costs of Denbo's "letting out" from his other expenses to the town: William Willee received £2 5s for "supporting" Denbo. Next, Samuel Willee "maintained" Denbo with "Shoes Stockings and other Necessaries" for £15 13s 5d. Daniel Davis was paid £2 8s for "Shirting" for Denbo. Finally, William Willee again was paid £1 5s "for Attendance and Necessaries for Salathiel Denbo when he was Sick."[40] The money spent on "letting out" a town pauper was not necessarily meant to cover clothing or medical costs. The records for

Lee and Madbury also confirm this. There were, however, town paupers who were not "let out" to a fellow townsman but who did receive poor relief.

In Durham, Nehemiah Pitman received clothing worth £6 in 1755. The following year Durham spent £5 on "Sundrys Supplyd" Pitman before he was "bid off" to Benjamin Mathes in 1757.[41] Gehabond(?) Bodge of Lee delivered $1.30 worth of beef to Widow Furnald in February, 1812. Edward B. Nealley delivered $6.07 worth of firewood in March of that year.[42] Selectman Abraham Clark of Madbury was paid $5.29 for "necessaries for James Bishops [sic] wife when She had a little one while said James was in Dover jail" in 1807.[43]

The Revolutionary War caused a discernible shift in the administration and availability of poor relief. During the war there was a shortage of supplies and rampant inflation. Some families were faced with poverty because the man of the house had enlisted and thus deprived the family farm or business of its main support. The community had to shoulder additional duties: Samuel Mathes of Lee was chosen by vote to supply "the Souldiers Families" in 1779. In 1780 and 1781, it was Captain Reuben Hill's duty to do the same.[44] From 1777 through 1781, Durham expended large amounts of money to supply the soldiers' families. Poor relief expenditures are listed for Madbury during these years, but none of them are described as arising from the war.

Because of the disruptions of war, poor relief briefly escaped the confines of town jurisdiction. Three petitions to the New Hampshire state legislature from Durham and Lee illustrate this point; these were individual cases and all related to men serving in the Continental Army. The two Durham petitions were addressed to the Council and the House of Representatives. The first one concerned David Copps and is dated January 7, 1777. The unfortunate former wheelwright "received a Shot in the Knee, which he Can't have Extracted." He lost his clothes and $30.50 in getting home from Lake Champlain. Because he was unable to work, the petition claimed him to be "Reduced to the lowest Ebb of poverty, that he Can't procure the Necessaries of Life, for himself, wife, & two Children." Likewise, widow Sarah Adams petitioned the same legislative bodies for aid in September, 1777, describing herself as "a helpless widow destitute of the means of procuring a Livelihood as her sold dependence was on her Husbands pay." Both Copps and Adams received state aid.[45] In the third case, Susanna Crown of

Durham, who had lost her husband in the war in 1779, received $20.00 in aid from the town.[46] Perhaps her husband had been a member of the local militia, thus making his survivors eligible for compensation from the town.

In Lee, the process of relief for Edward Dearborn was slightly convoluted. Dearborn's brother-in-law, Samuel Snell, petitioned the General Court in 1778 for aid since Dearborn "came to your petitioners house in distressed Circumstances, a Musket Ball had pierced thro' his arm above the elbow, he was poor, without money or Friend to assist him." The state consented to paying the $16.00 owed Dr. Marshall of Lee for attending the unfortunate Dearborn.[47]

The town also assumed responsibility at times for relieving the distress of those citizens who had lost their homes and possessions because of fire. Like smallpox, fire was a fairly common disaster which could strike anyone. Unfortunately the records say very little about fire relief. Lieutenant Benjamin Chesley of Durham was excused from paying his taxes in 1789 "on account of his misfortune by fire."[48] In late 1802, the town of Portsmouth suffered heavy damage from a fire. Both Lee and Durham made efforts to help in January, 1803. Both towns initially proposed to tax themselves in order to raise money to help Portsmouth, and both proposals were defeated. Instead, the townspeople voted to raise money for Portsmouth fire victims by voluntary subscriptions.[49] This is a rare instance of towns helping each other to relieve distressed citizens.

More often, poor relief was a source of discord between towns. Just as towns expected to govern themselves, they expected to take care of their own paupers. A perusal of the records shows that disagreements over relieving nonresident paupers were common throughout the period under study. Since towns were liable for the expenses incurred by their paupers, legal provisions were made to restrict their settlement. As far back as 1679, New Hampshire made efforts to define residence qualifications. A three-month period of residence was required before the newcomer could be considered an inhabitant and so be entitled to poor relief.[50] That is, if the newcomer was not "warned out" first.

Settlement laws became stricter as time went on. The time necessary to establish inhabitancy was extended from three months to twelve months in 1771.[51] "An Act to Ascertain the Ways & Means By Which Persons May Gain a Settlement In Any Town or District Within This State So As To Entitle Them to Support Therein If They Shall Be Poor and Unable to Support Themselves" was passed in

1796. It listed eight conditions by which settlement status could be acquired. For example, a person could gain settlement if he were age twenty-one or older, had real estate worth $250 in the town, and had paid poll and estate taxes for four consecutive years. A woman was considered an inhabitant of the town in which her husband had settlement. One could also achieve settlement by being a legitimate child of a person having settlement status. These are just three out of the eight possible conditions.[52] There were some modifications of this law in 1816, 1828, 1842, and 1878, but it remained essentially unchanged throughout the nineteenth century.

The "warning out" process, described in Chapter I, was practiced in Durham, Lee, and Madbury. The first "warning out" on record took place in Madbury in 1762, when Constable Joseph Daniels was paid £6 3s "for carrying Rachel Jonson out of ye Parrish & warning Sundry Persons to Remove out of the Same."[53] Judging from the available evidence, Madbury had the most occasion to "warn out" potential town charges and Durham had the least. Sometimes "warning out" did not always work. Back in 1776, Constable John Snell of Lee was ordered to "warn out" Mariam Clemons.[54] He did so, but she somehow managed to slip through and become a Lee resident who was maintained as a town pauper for at least twenty years.

A wide variety of people were "warned out." Single women and men, children, women with bastard children, and entire families were "warned out" in Durham, Lee, and Madbury. John Hill of Madbury had his hands full when he "warned out" Benjamin Leathers and his family (who also managed to become town paupers like Mariam Clemons in Lee), a "negro man by the Name of Peter Caleb Follet & family," Samuel Sloper and his family, and Reuben Cook and his family in 1792.[55]

Quite a few disputes took place among the three towns, and with Dover, Newmarket, Barrington, Northwood, Nottingham, Rochester, Gilmanton, Boscawen, and other towns. A typical record entry says that Edward Wells of Madbury was paid $1.50 in 1799 to notify the Dover selectmen to settle the dispute over which town was to maintain Anna Stevenson.[56] There were a number of cases when one town billed another for medical expenses when a nonresident pauper required treatment. Starting in 1808, Durham had to pay Madbury for the expenses incurred by Eli Demeritt "since he Broak his arm." Madbury billed Durham for Demeritt's care in 1808, 1810, and 1811.[57] Lee had to pay Joshua Drew of Nottingham $4.17

in 1804 for clothing Mary Clemmons.[58]

Numerous entries for medical relief for paupers can be found throughout the town records. Sometimes the "letting out" agreement specified that the town was to pay separately for medical expenses incurred. In other cases medical care seems to have been afforded by the town as needed, while those boarding paupers were paid for "nursing" or "caring" for them. There are also records of payments made to the local doctor for "doctoring the poor" for a given year.

Albert Deutsch asserts that medical care for all of a town's poor might be delegated to one doctor.[59] There are sufficient entries in the records to indicate that this was practiced here too from time to time. Dr. Adams of Durham received £7 10s "for Doctring the poor" in 1755, a typical example of this practice.[60] There are numerous examples for Lee and Durham. Madbury seems to have relied less heavily on doctors for treating town paupers; its records contain occasional references to doctors, but more often a sick pauper was cared for by a fellow citizen. In 1793 James Pinkham Jr. of Madbury was paid £1 16s for the support and nursing of Abigail Thomas "in her laying in with a Bastard Child." In 1796 Stephen Hanson was paid $8.42 for supporting the son of James Johnson "in Sickness at his House."[61]

A common entry in the records of all three towns is for medical supplies furnished by private citizens to sick paupers. Often the supplies are described as "necessaries," a term which could cover anything from basic everyday items like firewood to medical supplies. Maul Hanson of Madbury supplied Ruben Chesley "in Sickness" with three quarts and a pint of rum in 1789.[62] In 1820, Gardner Towle of Lee was paid $37.32 "for supplies &c in Thomas Rollins Sickness with Broken Arm."[63] Going back to 1753, we find Benjamin Mathes of Durham supplying £1 4s worth of rum and sugar for Mary Denbo.[64] At several other points in the records we find wine, brandy, or rum supplied to sick paupers.

Even in death paupers cost the towns money. In many instances the expense is simply listed as "funeral" or "burial." Nathaniel Hill of Durham was paid £1 1s "for the Wid.ʷ Betty Davis' funeral" in 1770.[65] A more informative description is found in the Madbury *Treasurer's Record 1755-1826* for the funeral of John Pinkham in 1775. Two gallons of rum were consumed at the funeral and John Demerit received £1 6s for "Cofen Shurt & sheet for to Bury sd Pinkham."[66] Expenses for burying cloths, winding sheets, coffins, and funeral attendance can be found in Lee's records too. Most likely, pauper funerals tended to be paltry affairs compared to those of wealthier townsmen.

Many town medical expenses are related to smallpox. Since the appearance of smallpox was something of an emergency, makeshift measures were taken. Oftentimes the patient was treated as usual, but because of the contagious nature of smallpox, special provisions had to be made by the town. Efforts were made to isolate the disease by quarantining smallpox sufferers.[67] Durham was afflicted by the pox in 1761, and at least two citizens were paid by the town for the use of their houses. Widow Mary Critchet was paid £6 5s for the use of her home, while John Stevenson was paid £3 15s "for cleansing it" of the contagion. Durham also paid John Leighton "for cleansing those houses Infected with the Small Pox."[68] Smallpox relief did not exclusively concern the town poor. Because of the serious nature of an outbreak of smallpox, the town took the financial burden of handling this disease upon itself and paid for the care of citizens who were not necessarily paupers. Similar measures were taken in Lee and Madbury.

Lee and especially Madbury had quite a few unwed mothers to maintain. Most often, the town had to pay the costs of medical care for the pregnant woman and then find a home for her and the child. In at least two cases, Madbury was able to bring suit against the father of the illegitimate child. Abigail Thomas cost Madbury £1 6s in 1793 and $18.82 in 1796 by giving birth to two illegitimate children. In 1796 the selectmen were able to "prosecute and carry on an action against Moses Woodman for the maintenance of Abigail Thomas Bastard Child." In 1803 Selectman Abraham Clark "settled with Benjamin Jackson for his Bastard Child."[69]

Who were the town paupers? How many were there? It is very difficult to say exactly who the paupers were, and even how many there were, due to the nature of the records. Usually all one can find is a pauper's name and his expense to the town. The pauper's age is rarely mentioned. There are indirect clues such as the description of someone as "son of" or "poor child." If a man or woman is maintained along with his or her children, one has an indication that the parent is middle-aged or younger in most cases. Quite a few widows were paupers, which indicates that a significant portion of the town poor were older women. If a single man is listed, his age is usually impossible to determine unless he has a wife and children. Since there are entries for sick male and female paupers and their funeral expenses, there may have been a large number of elderly paupers. Some people enter the record only as sick paupers. Perhaps the illness or injury was the cause of their pauperism. This certainly was true for David Copps of Durham and Edward Dearborn of Lee, who were wounded in the Revolutionary War.

Along with people who were only temporarily town paupers, there were certain individuals and families who became permanent paupers. The Denbo or Denmore family of Durham was constantly maintained throughout the 1750s and '60s. They seem to have been established as paupers from the start of the records, like Widow Drisco. At other points a pauper family enters the records with just one or two individuals needing assistance. One such example is the Elliot family of Lee. They appeared in 1804 when Molly Elliot was "warned out." In 1810 Nathaniel Elett, Namey Elett, and "the wd of Robard Elot and two Children" were "bid off."[70] During the next few years Sarrah Ellot, Mark Elliot, and Widow Comfort Elliot were all "let out" too. Other pauper families who were maintained for years in Lee were the Runnels or Reynolds family, the Glovers, the Rollins family, the Clays, the Harts, and especially the Leathers family. All three towns had to maintain various members of the Leathers family.

Sometimes the more prosperous members of the Leathers family maintained other paupers, even to the extent of maintaining each other. Patience Leathers of Lee was paid $5.84 in 1815 for "keeping" Lois Leathers' child.[71] It was not unusual for the town to pay a citizen to maintain one of his own poor relatives. In 1794 Samuel Pinkham of Madbury was paid £6 19s for keeping, supporting, and washing the sick Moses Pinkham.[72] The existence of problem families and of individuals who remain on the lists for many years as town paupers indicates that the town government could nearly always count on having to spend some proportion of its annual budget on poor relief. Factors such as health were important too, since much of the relief expense was related to medical costs.

The pauper populations of Durham, Lee, and Madbury gradually increased during the period from the early eighteenth through early nineteenth centuries. Until approximately 1790, Durham and Madbury maintained around five paupers each per year. Lee's records are very incomplete until 1801. Durham's records do not provide much detail on individual paupers after 1806, so it is difficult to say just how many paupers were maintained yearly for the rest of the pre-almshouse period in that town. For Lee and Madbury, the period from 1800 to 1830 was one of a slowly increasing pauper population. Most of the time, a dozen or more paupers were maintained yearly. During this period Lee's population increased slightly from 978 in 1800 to 1009 in 1830, while Madbury's dropped from 544 in 1800 to 510 in 1830. In contrast, Durham's population rose noticeably, from 1126 inhabitants in 1800 to 1606 in 1830.[73]

The number of town paupers increased gradually over this period in all three towns. The amount of money expended per year on poor relief between the 1750s and 1830s is not a very helpful indicator of poor relief trends. Such factors as missing data, extreme wartime inflation, and currency changes have to be considered. Thus, when annual poor relief expenditures are plotted on a graph, there are sometimes wild fluctuations from one year to another while the number of paupers on relief is actually unchanged. Durham's annual poor relief expenditures between 1751 and 1834 can be described as follows: a sharp rise from around £20 per year in 1751 to over £460 each year in 1764, which was around 10% of annual town expenditures; and a gradual decline between 1766 and 1775 with expenses at about £50 per year. This ranged from 67.53% of Durham's entire budget in 1767 to only 8.33% in 1776. Usually poor relief hovered at around 30% of the budget during this decade. For the period between 1776 and 1819, Dyrham's data are unreliable and incomplete, showing a few wild fluctuations. It is interesting to note that the annual expenditures in the fifteen years prior to the town poor farm show a sharp decline from $995 per year to about $390 per year in 1834. As a percentage of annual town expenditures, poor relief stayed mostly close to 20% (see Appendix, Table I).

Two possible reasons for this decline are suggested. First, the competition started by Ezekial Twombly to bid for all the town poor in one lot probably depressed prices. Second, as Americans moved West, they began to exploit rich new agricultural resources, making New England farming a less profitable business. Thus, the value of town paupers as agricultural laborers may have been in decline.

The picture is less confused for Lee between 1801 and 1837. This town's poor relief expenditures show a gradual but jagged upward trend from around $120 per year to around $500 per year. A gigantic leap in 1838 was mainly due to the $2000 spent on purchasing Lee's poor farm. As a percentage of annual town expenditures, Lee's poor relief between 1801 and 1837 was very uneven. This was probably a result of the semi-annual terms of payment in the "letting out" system. Most of the time poor relief constituted between 12% and 20% of the annual town expenditure. This is a lower figure than Durham's from 1819 to 1834, but the trend was similar: expenses were relatively stable and possibly declining (see Appendix, Table II).

Finally, changes from old to new tenor and wild wartime inflation have to be considered in Madbury's annual poor relief costs from 1756 to 1794. From 1756 through 1766, poor relief was roughly £150 to £200 a year, which was about 5% to 10% of all Madbury's annual expenditures. Discounting the inflation of 1777-1780, Madbury's annual poor bill (in new tenor pounds) showed a gradual increase from around £5 per year in the late 1760s to around £35 per year in the early 1790s. In terms of the town's total annual expenses, this upward trend was not the case. Poor relief accounted for about 10% of town expenses in the late 1760s and declined to a fairly constant 2% to 3% in the 1780s and early '90s. A sharp increase in the late 1790s to $290, followed by a decrease to the $100-per-year range in the early 1800s, was followed by a very sharp increase to the $400- to $450-range in the period between 1814 and 1820. In turn, this was followed by a sharp decrease to the $150 range and less in the 1820s. As a percentage of town expenditures, there were very sharp variations, from nearly 40% in 1795 to only about 8% in 1827. Very roughly, the trend in Madbury was a gradual increase from around 20% each year in the period from 1800 to 1810 to around 30% from 1810 to 1818, and then a gradual decline to less than 20% in the following decade (see Appendix, Table III).

Apparently poor relief was not a fixed part of these towns' budgets. In both absolute terms and as a percentage of annual town expenditures, poor relief costs varied widely. It appears that poor relief expenses were regarded as an unknown factor by Durham officials. One of many such entries is the notice to Andrew Simpson, constable and tax collector in 1803, that he is to pay to the selectmen "the residue or remainder" of the entire town budget. It was to be used "for the support of the poor of said Town and other contingencies."[74]

In Lee's *Daybooks*, the amount bid for the town poor was much less than what was actually spent. Old pauper bills had to be paid. Medical and clothing expenses added a lot, "outdoor" relief was unpredictable, and there was always an uncertainty as to just how many town paupers there would be in the coming year; despite "warning out," new paupers did make their appearance. The town was also liable for expenses incurred by its own paupers who wandered into neighboring areas. Finally, there were the added expenses of people who became ill, orphaned, or paupers in the middle of the year, after the annual "letting out" of town paupers in the spring. Provisions had to be made for these people, too.

The only conclusion about the expenses of "letting out" the poor in these three towns is that in the period from 1750 to 1800, yearly maintenance costs were between £5 and £20 for a typical pauper; and that in the period from 1800 to 1830 the costs tended to be about $15 to $30 per year for a typical pauper.

These figures are admittedly imprecise, due to several factors. First there is the incompleteness of the records. Second, the costs vary so greatly because there were currency changes, and, during the Revolutionary War, a period of extreme inflation. A third consideration is the widely differing conditions of the poor, who ranged from children to old widows and from healthy strong men to sickly people; and differing conditions means differing expenses. The fourth factor further complicates matters: the additional entries for "outdoor" relief afforded to both paupers already "let out" and those paupers still maintaining their own residence. Thus, in calculating poor relief as the percentage of annual town expenditures, it is practically impossible to separate "outdoor" relief from the cost of "letting out" the poor and from medical expenses.

The available evidence suggests that Durham, Lee, and Madbury fit the typical eighteenth- and early nineteenth-century pattern of poor relief administration described in Chapter I. Since they were small towns, they had no almshouse, although Durham did toy with the idea in 1762. The "outdoor" system of relief prevailed instead. Indigent or sick citizens were sometimes maintained in their own homes, with the town paying for items like clothing, food, medicines, and firewood. Most often, town paupers were "let out" to the lowest bidder. Children were frequently "bound out." For both adult and child paupers, written contracts or indentures ensured the rights and duties of both the paupers and those taking them in. Undesirable strangers and nonresident potential paupers were "warned out" of town. Overseers of the poor (who were frequently also the selectmen in Durham, Lee, and Madbury) were elected to administer and supervise poor relief.

All three towns experienced sharp fluctuations in poor relief expenditures during the period under study. Incomplete data, currency changes, and inflation account for some of this. Unexpected expenses added their share when new paupers appeared, when the smallpox struck, or when a man died leaving a widow and children.

As has been seen, poor relief was a local concern. Durham, Lee, and Madbury were very reluctant to care for nonresident paupers. In turn, they were obliged to pay when one of their own paupers incurred bills in other towns.

Durham and Lee followed the national trend when they switched from "outdoor" relief to "indoor" relief in the 1830s; in contrast, there was no town poor farm built in Madbury. Several motives for change are suggested: the unpredictability of "outdoor" relief costs, due mainly to the unpredictable occurrences of disease and injury; the decline in value of agricultural labor in New Hampshire at a time when the rich farm lands to the West were being settled; publicity about the benefits of "indoor" relief propagated by social reformers all over America; and changes in the local economy which made "outdoor" relief unworkable.

Along with the decline in agriculture, there was a simultaneous expansion in industrialization. Textile mills came to New England in the early nineteenth century. New Hampshire's economy was noticeably affected by this development, as will be seen in the next chapter.

All of these changes contributed to the establishment of town poor farms in Durham and Lee. There is some indication that Madbury continued to rely on the "letting out" system long after Durham and Lee had largely abandoned it.

NOTES TO CHAPTER II

1. *First Census of the United States* (Philadelphia, 1791), 14.

2. *Ibid.*, 9-10.

3. Albert S. Batchellor, ed., *Laws of New Hampshire*, 1 (Manches-

ter, N.H., 1904), 526-527.

4. *Ibid.*, 219-220.

5. *Ibid.*, 254-255.

6. *Lee Town Records 1766-1815* (copied 1901-1902), 2.

7. *Copy of the Town Records of the Town of Durham, N.H., 1732-1841*, 2 Original Part 1 1739-1793 (copied 1942-1945), 55 and 60.

8. Irvin G. Wyllie, "The Search for an American Law of Charity, 1776-1844," *Mississippi Valley Historical Review*, 46 (1959), 205.

9. *Town of Durham, 1732-1841*, 2, Part 1, 44-45.

10. Marcus W. Jernegan, *Laboring and Dependent Classes in Colonial America 1607-1783* (New York, 1965), 116.

11. Batchellor, ed., *Laws of New Hampshire*, 2 (Concord, N.H., 1913), 343.

12. *Town of Durham, 1732-1841*, I 1732-1739 (copied 1942), 77.

13. *Ibid.*, 77.

14. *Town of Durham, 1732-1841*, 2, Part 1, 21.

15. Madbury -- Miscellaneous Town Papers 1768-1799, New Hampshire Historical Society, Concord, N.H.

16. *Record of Payments and Receipts: Daybook 1802-1809*, I, 70.

17. *Payment Book 1809-1825*, 48.

18. "Contracts Respecting the Poor of Durham From April 1798," *Records on Paupers and Wharfs, 1798-1806*.

19. Benjamin J. Klebaner, "Pauper Auctions: The 'New England Method' of Poor Relief," *Essex Institute Historical Collections*, 91 (1955), 204.

20. Batchellor, ed., *Laws of New Hampshire*, 2, 269.

21. Henry H. Metcalf, ed., *Laws of New Hampshire*, 3 (Bristol, N.H., 1915), 390-391.

22. *Town of Durham Accounts 1751-1782*, 4.

23. *Lee Town Records 1766-1815*, 17.

24. *Memorandum Book for 1784 and 1785*, 2.

25. *Town Book. Treasurer's Record 1755-1826.*

26. Madbury -- Miscellaneous Papers.

27. *Ibid.*

28. "Contracts," *Records on Paupers and Wharfs*, 1.

29. *Daybook 1802-1809*, I, 7.

30. Madbury -- Miscellaneous Papers.

31. *Daybook 1802-1809*, I, 9.

32. *Treasurer's Record 1755-1826.*

33. *Durham Accounts 1751-1782*, 40.

34. *Payment Book 1809-1825*, 86.

35. "Contracts," *Records on Paupers and Wharfs*, 5-30.

36. *Payment Book 1809-1825*, 65.

37. *Town of Durham, 1732-1841, 3 Original. March 14, 1809 - Nov. 1820* (copied 1945-1946), 195.

38. *Ibid., 4 Original. Oct. 21, 1820 - March 29, 1832*, 32 and 53.

39. *Payment Book 1809-1825*, 142 and 145.

40. *Durham Accounts 1751-1782*, 4.

41. *Ibid.*, 22, 24, and 26.

42. *Payment Book 1809-1825*, 30 and 33.

43. *Treasurer's Record 1755-1826*.

44. *Lee Town Records 1766-1815*, 64, 70, and 77.

45. Isaac Hammond, ed., *Town Papers: Documents Relating to Towns in New Hampshire*, XI (Concord, N.H., 1882), 588 and 596.

46. *Town of Durham, 1732-1841*, 2, Part 1, 94.

47. Hammond, ed., *Town Papers: Documents Relating to Towns in New Hampshire*, XII (Concord, N.H., 1883), 390.

48. *Town of Durham, 1732-1841*, 2, Part 1, 139.

49. *Ibid.*, 2, Part 2 1793-1808 (copied 1942-1945), 202 and *Lee Town Records 1766-1815*, 298.

50. Batchellor, ed., *Laws of New Hampshire*, 1, 36.

51. Josiah H. Benton, *Warning Out in New England* (Boston, 1911), 115.

52. Edwin C. Bean, ed., *Laws of New Hampshire*, 6 (Concord, N.H., 1917), 299-301.

53. *Treasurer's Record 1755-1826*.

54. *Lee Town Records 1766-1815*, 339.

55. *Treasurer's Record 1755-1826*.

56. *Ibid.*

57. *Ibid.*

58. *Daybook 1802-1809*, I, 31.

59. Albert Deutsch, "The Sick Poor in Colonial Times," *American Historical Review*, 46 (1941), 577.

60. *Durham Accounts 1751-1782*, 22.

61. *Treasurer's Record 1755-1826*.

62. *Ibid.*

63. *Payment Book 1809-1825*, 127.

64. *Durham Accounts 1751-1782*, 17.

65. *Ibid.*

66. *Treasurer's Record 1755-1826*.

67. Deutsch, "Sick Poor," *AHR*, 46 (1941), 565.

68. *Durham Accounts 1751-1782*, 35.

69. *Treasurer's Record 1755-1826*.

70. *Payment Book 1809-1825*, 10-11.

71. *Ibid.*, 59.

72. *Treasurer's Record 1755-1826*.

73. See *Return of the Whole Number of Persons Within the Districts of the United States, According to "An Act providing for the second census or Enumeration of the Inhabitants of the United States"* (Washington, 1801), 4 and *Fifth Census, or Enumeration of the Inhabitants of the United States in 1830* (Washington, 1832), 10-11.

74. *Town of Durham 1732-1841*, 2 Part 2, 212.

CHAPTER III

The Town Farm System

The decades from 1830 through 1890 were a time of economic and political expansion throughout the United States, yet the populations of Durham, Lee, and Madbury suffered a decline over this period. It is likely the effects of the depressions of 1857-1858 and 1873-1879 were felt here as elsewhere. Possibly the Civil War was a factor, too, since it caused economic disruptions and increased taxes.

The most likely explanation for the decreasing poor farm population is that it was a reflection of the general population decline in this area. Strafford County suffered stagnation and decline in the middle of the nineteenth century. As new counties were created out of the old ones in the 1840s, Strafford County shrank from 61,127 people in 1840 to 29,374 in 1850.[1] The county actually suffered a loss of population during the 1860s when it declined from 31,493 inhabitants in 1860 to 30,243 in 1870. By 1890 it had grown, but only to 35,442 inhabitants.[2]

Durham, Lee, and Madbury followed suit. At first Durham's population increased from 1498 people in 1840 to 1534 in 1860. Thereafter it declined rapidly; by 1890 there were only 871 people living in Durham. Lee declined from 926 in 1840 to 606 in 1890, while Madbury was reduced from 489 people in 1840 to 367 in 1890.[3] Other towns such as Barrington and Middleton declined too, since their economies were largely dependent on agriculture.[4]

Starting in 1850, the United States government began to keep statistics on pauperism. Until 1880 the information is no more specific than the number of paupers on the national and state levels.

The figures are based on the number of inmates in asylums and almshouses, the number of people "receiving in any form and in any degree" relief money or supplies.[5] Keeping the instability of these figures in mind, the national trend was a massive increase from 134,972 paupers in 1850 to 321,655 in 1860; followed by a sharp decrease in 1870 to only 116,102 paupers in the entire United States. At the same time, New Hampshire jumped from 3600 paupers in 1850 to 4394 in 1860, and fell to only 2636 paupers in 1870.[6]

The entire population of the United States was 23,191,876 in 1850; 31,443,321 in 1860; and 39,818,449 in 1870.[7] Thus, paupers were 0.58% of the population in 1830; 1.02% in 1860; and down to 0.28% in 1870. The entire population of New Hampshire was 317,976 people in 1850; 326,073 in 1860; and 318,300 in 1870.[8] In 1850 1.13% of New Hampshire's population was classified as paupers, twice as many as that for the United States as a whole. In 1860, 1.34% of New Hampshire's inhabitants were paupers. This was a slight increase and was close to the national proportion of 1.02%. While the United States' general population grew between 1860 and 1870, that of New Hampshire declined slightly. So did its number of paupers: by 1870, they were 0.83% of the population. This was a decline, but not as dramatic as the decline in the number of paupers for the entire United States, which was down to 0.28% of the population.

One would expect there to be an increase in pauperism between 1860 and 1870 because of the disruptions and privations caused by the Civil War, especially in the South. However, New Hampshire followed the national trend in this case, too. Perhaps the economic depression of 1857-1858 was partly responsible for the vast increase in people classified as paupers in the census of 1860. Even though the entire country was affected by this depression, it was the Eastern urban areas which suffered most.[9] Thus, the apparent decline in the poor farm populations of Durham and Lee between 1860 and 1870 fits into the larger picture. The state and national increase apparent between 1850 and 1860 cannot be compared to the situation in Durham, Lee, and Madbury, because the original sources are incomplete.

Several possible reasons for the decline in the populations of Durham, Lee, and Madbury in the nineteenth century can be suggested. Industrialization was appearing in New Hampshire at this time, in the form of textile mills. While New Hampshire's population as a whole increased, this increase was taking place in the mill towns such as Newmarket, Dover, Somersworth, and Rochester. Both countrymen and foreign immigrants moved to the mill towns to find work. As a result, two important economic bases suffered in the nineteenth century: ship building and farming. As ship building and shipping declined in the areas north of Boston, so did the economies of towns which had profited from this industry. This was partly due to new transportation lines created by innovations such as canals, railroads, and steamboats, which linked New York City to the vast, expanding interior regions of America. Associated industries such as lumbering and ropemaking declined too. Farming suffered greatly during the nineteenth century.

Mills were established in Newmarket, Dover, Somersworth, and Rochester. All of these towns experienced great population growth in the nineteenth century, some of which must have come from Durham, Lee, and Madbury's decline: residents were leaving the farm towns to work in the mill towns. In Newmarket, Stephen Hanson founded the Newmarket Manufacturing Company in 1823, the first of several cotton mills. Throughout the 1820s and 1830s, Newmarket's population grew as other mills were built.[10]

Spectacular growth took place in Dover soon after the Dover Cotton Factory was established in 1812. Known as the Cocheco Manufacturing Company from 1827, it eventually covered twenty-five acres, held 130,000 spindles and 2800 looms, and employed over two thousand workers.[11] In 1824 Alfred I. Sawyer established the Sawyer Woolen Mills, adding to Dover's prosperity. Other industries were located in Dover, whose population grew from 2870 in 1820 to 5449 just ten years later.[12] Somersworth, too, started its expansion in 1823 with the Great Falls Manufacturing Company.[13] Finally, Eliphalet Horne brought the woolen industry to Rochester in 1811. Blankets were produced by several Rochester companies. Franklin McDuffee comments that the Gonic Manufacturing Company (established in 1838), "gives employment to hundreds in other vocations, makes a home market for the products of the farm and shop, stimulates other industries, and increases the population."[14]

But population suffered in Durham, Lee, and Madbury not just from these industrial developments. As the rich new soils of the West were exploited, the New Hampshire farmer was forced out of business. Vast quantities of produce from the West, shipped at cheap rates to the East, proved to be too much competition for many farmers.[15] Agricultural towns like Durham, Lee, and Madbury were affected. Many farmers were forced to give up and move to the cities to find work, or join the settlers who were opening up the West. The sons and daughters of Durham, Lee, and Madbury left their towns, which were on the way to becoming depressed backwater villages.

Thus, poverty itself was not in decline but rather the regional population as a whole was decreasing. With a declining number of paupers on the town farm, "indoor" relief may have been getting too expensive to be worthwhile. But it was also less worthwhile than previously for a family to board town paupers. Not only was there a diminishing value in agricultural labor, and therefore a diminishing need for extra hands, but changed social attitudes may have also contributed to the reluctance of families to take in the town poor. Distaste and fear had by and large replaced the sympathy and the old feeling of social obligation.

This chapter will describe the local almshouse system from its start in the 1830s to its demise in the 1860s and 1870s. Poor relief in Madbury for this period will be only briefly described, for this town had no poor farm and there are very few original source materials available for this time period in any case. Using the available evidence, we will examine the transition from "outdoor" to "indoor" relief in Durham and Lee. Annual reports and town meeting minutes will be analyzed for details on how the town poor farms operated. Fortunately, there exists a very informative town farm inventory and appraisal for Lee, covering the years 1859 to 1873.

The new system of "indoor" relief became popular in the United States in the 1830s. Various reasons have been suggested as to why communities began to rely on the almshouse system at this time. Robert H. Bremner, Samuel Mencher, and David J. Rothman stress the new visibility of poverty in America. Poverty was now viewed with alarm; there seemed to be no end in sight; and the presence of large numbers of indigent people in the land of opportunity seemed unnatural. The poor themselves were frequently blamed for their condition. Sophonisba P. Breckinridge and James Leiby describe how reformers attacked the problem of poverty through the implementation of almshouses. Rothman describes how the almshouse was hailed as the perfect solution to poverty: paupers could be concentrated in one location and then be systematically rehabilitated into self-sufficient citizens.

The reforming motive of "indoor" relief is just a partial explanation for its implementation in Durham and Lee. The generally terse accounts in the records of Durham, Lee, and Madbury provide a fair amount of factual information, but it is not easy to explain just why Durham and Lee switched from "outdoor" to "indoor" relief in 1834 and 1838, respectively. Other factors which helped determine the issue may have been the unpredictable nature of "outdoor" relief expenses, a decline in the value of agricultural labor (making it less worthwhile for a farmer to board paupers in his own home), and changes in the local economy, notably the coming of the textile industry to this area.

Although it was not until 1832 that the town of Durham decided to purchase a poor farm, there is an entry referring to "the poor house" in records from 1829.[16] It is likely that this is a reference to the house of the person boarding the paupers all in one lot. The poor were still being "let out" to the lowest bidder and continued to be so until 1834. Since this is the only entry for a "poor house" before 1832, it would probably be inaccurate to consider this as more than a temporary or partial measure, especially since "outdoor" relief was still in full swing.

The switch from "outdoor" to "indoor" relief was not a sudden occurrence in either Durham or Lee. It took over two years of petitions and meetings in Durham, while in Lee the process began in 1830 and was not completed until 1839. Even then, the records indicate that Durham and Lee continued to rely partially on "outdoor" relief after their poor farms were in full operation.

The origins of the Durham poor farm are interesting. Seven townsmen presented a petition to the Durham selectmen on March 29, 1832. The petitioners asked the selectmen to let the town vote on whether Durham ought to sell the town wharves, buildings, and real estate, and use the money from the sales "to purchase a farm for the purpose of supporting the poor of said town."[17] This might be a reflection of the economic changes of the period, when ship building and agriculture were in decline while textile manufacturing was taking over. After voting on the matter at three town meetings, a committee consisting of Benjamin Thompson, Daniel Chesley, and William J. Chesley was chosen to sell "town lots or parsonage lands in said Durham" (but not the town wharves and building yards) for the purpose of purchasing a town poor farm.[18]

John Haven of Portsmouth sold "three certain tracts or parcels of Land with the buildings thereon situate" to the town of Durham on December 14, 1832, for $2233.56. On March 12, 1833, the town voted to raise $300.00 to buy the remaining twelve and a quarter acres out of an original one hundred from John Haven for the town poor farm.[19]

In 1833 Captain Edward Griffiths kept the Durham poor for $470.00.[20] The poor farm was bought and paid for in 1833, but there were two obstacles yet to be overcome. Some Durham residents looked upon the poor farm as an unprofitable purchase. Benjamin Mathes, Jr., tried to convince the town to get rid of it but his motion was defeated.[21] A greater obstacle was the fact that the farm buildings were in sad condition. So in January, 1834, another committee was created, this time to decide on the necessary repairs and how much they would cost. On February 14, 1834, the thirteen-member committee presented a report on the repairs thought necessary:

> "the town should erect a building agreeable to the following dimentions [sic]: a two story building 27 by 29 feet, to be placed on the west end of the house now on the farm. To finish the lower story and the second story to be left unfinished except to lay the garret floor with a good cellar under the whole. Also to shingle the whole or a part of the old house and clapboard the smae [sic] and put it in good repair, the whole of which we think can be done in season for the reception of the poor by the 8th. of April next and do believe that the whole can be done for four or five hundred dollars."[22]

Yet another committee was chosen to contract out these repairs to the lowest bidder. Captain Mark Willey agreed to build the new addition for $487.00 and Samuel P. Chesley got the cellar job for $34.25.[23] Durham's town poor farm opened its doors on April 8, 1834. Benjamin Kelly was elected superintendent.

The implementation of "indoor" relief in Lee was fully as complicated and took much longer. As far back as 1830 a town poor farm had been proposed at town meetings.[24] Over the next seven years, the voters of Lee argued about this idea. Almost every year the farm was put on the warrant and then dismissed. At the same time, the citizens of Lee debated the question of how the town would support the poor for the following year.

Most likely the reason that the town debated the question of poor relief throughout the 1830s was that the old forms of "outdoor" relief were no longer satisfactory. In 1830 the town voted to "let out" the poor to one man (as Durham had been doing since 1819); in 1833 this measure was dropped and the poor were "let out" individually as before.[25] A committee was even formed to investigate the purchase of a poor farm in 1832.

Lee finally decided on a poor farm in 1836. A committee consisting of Gardner Towle, George Lang, Joseph S. Lawrence Jr., Simon Otis, and Josiah Bartlett was authorized to "make enquiries" about purchasing a farm. By March 14, 1837, the town had definitely decided to buy a poor farm. Money to pay for the farm was to be raised from surplus revenue. If this was not enough, the selectmen were to "higher [sic] the rest of it, on the faith and credit of the town."[26]

Samuel Jones sold his 112-acre farm to the town of Lee for $2000 on October 19, 1837. An additional acre and a half were purchased from James B. Creighton of Newmarket for $28 on September 14, 1839.[27] Even though furniture and supplies were far from adequate, and repairs were still needed (as in Durham's poor farm), the Lee town poor farm was opened in either late 1837 or early 1838. John S. Walker, overseer of the poor, was made superintendent of the farm in 1838.

Durham and Lee followed the national trend when they acquired poor farms in 1833 and 1837. For some years, leading social reformers had urged Americans to adopt the almshouse system of poor relief. One of the earliest proponents of "indoor" relief was Josiah Quincy, whose *Report of 1821 on the Pauper Laws of Massachusetts* pointed out the evils of "outdoor" relief and the supposed benefits of putting the poor in almshouses. Quincy and others maintained that by giving aid to paupers in their own homes, the public was, in effect, encouraging paupers to remain public charges. In turn, the presence of able-bodied idlers would tempt the laboring classes to quit working and acquire "habits of idleness, dissipation and extravagance."[28] The remedy, as Quincy and others saw it, was to put the poor to work in almshouses. Following European models and theories propounded by social reformers, many American communities incarcerated their paupers in almshouses in the 1820s and 1830s. Ideally, the poor were concentrated in one manageable group, kept out of mischief, productively employed, and thus were rehabilitated into honest working citizens who would fit into American society.

Few almshouses were so beneficial. Many towns made only the minimum effort to follow the new trend. Rural areas did not always have the resources to buy or construct an almshouse. Even when a small town decided to administer "indoor" relief, it was often forced to buy an old farm for the use of the poor, rather than construct a new facility.[29] Both Durham and Lee purchased ramshackle old farms for their poor. From the very beginning, as the old records show, Durham and Lee had to make repairs on the farm buildings to make them habitable.

Poor people had never been very popular but at least they had generally been regarded with some degree of compassion. Starting in the 1820s, a period of economic and political expansion, paupers were perceived to be abnormal and threatening. Thus one important component of the almshouse form of relief was its corrective or rehabilitative effort. Infirm or helpless paupers were still to be pitied, but institutional confinement was the best solution for them too. Almshouses were considered to be "houses of correction." They were akin to penitentiaries or reform schools in that the people confined there were to follow a routine of work and regulated living which was supposedly for their benefit. Thus, it is of considerable importance that Durham voted for its almshouse to be a house of correction in 1834.[30]

There were regulations in New Hampshire going as far back as the seventeenth century that directed overseers of the poor to set paupers to work in workhouses. The term "house of correction" first appears in a New Hampshire law of 1791. More relevant to the case of Durham is the 1828 law which describes the punitive aspect of the house of correction. Along with setting the inmates to work, the overseer was authorized to mete out the following punishments: hard labor, "parental correction," and solitary confinement for up to forty-eight hours. By this time, whipping was no longer legal.[31] Benjamin Kelly of Durham was given responsibility in 1834 "for the government of all persons sent there for correction and to establish necessary rules and regulations for ruling, governing, and punishing such persons as may be sent there."[32]

New Hampshire lawmakers committed a rather colorful cast of characters to the houses of correction if the laws on the subject may be taken as an indication. An 1828 statute called for the enclosure of:

> "all rogues, vagabonds, lewd, idle and disorderly persons, persons going about begging, persons using any subtle craft, juggling or unlawful games

or plays, persons pretending to have knowledge in physiognomy or palmistry, persons pretending that they can tell destinies or fortunes or discover by any spells or magic art where lost or stolen goods may be found, common pipers, fiddlers, runaways, stubborn servants or children, common drunkards, common night walkers, pilferers, persons wanton and lascivious in speech, conduct or behaviour, common railers or brawlers such as neglect their calling or employment, mispend [sic] what they earn and do not provide for the support of themselves and their families."[33]

There is evidence that Lee's poor farm also had a penal character. Poor farm superintendent John S. Walker was authorized "to take any measures to secure Benjamin Leathers and Jonathan Clay and any others who may abscond that he may think proper."[34] If town paupers were forbidden to "abscond" from the poor farm, their condition was comparable to that of prisoners or juvenile delinquents. Indeed, David J. Rothman observes that almshouse paupers were somewhere between patients and prisoners in status.[35]

This is not to say that paupers sent to the poor farm were any more constrained than those who had been "let out." Probably the same confinement existed, but it was the setting which was different. A pauper who was "let out" was obliged to work for his keep (unless he were infirm). It probably depended on the individual boarding the pauper as to how free a "let out" pauper was to come and go from his residence.

Whether or not Benjamin Leathers and Jonathan Clay were less or more free, the confinement of most of the town poor in one building was new. So too was the routine. The poor farm inmates had their days planned for them. Probably time was scheduled for moral instruction of some sort, since a house of correction was supposed to reform its inmates' characters. For example, Lee voted that the poor farm superintendent make arrangements with a minister to preach to the paupers, in 1840.[36] Life on the poor farms of Durham and Lee was regulated, and, for at least two Lee paupers, unpleasant.

Available sources such as annual reports and town farm inventories can give us a better picture of the poor farms. The annual reports of Durham, from the 1840s on, list itemized pauper expenses. There are a few such reports for Lee, but the main source of information on Lee's almshouse is the yearly inventory and appraisal of property on the farm, recorded from 1859 to 1873.

The first impression one receives upon viewing the town farm account in *Receipts & Expenditures of the Town of Durham, for the Year Ending Feb. 20, 1847* is that the farm provided employment for local citizens. Townsmen were paid for supplies and labor. Merchants and tailors did business with the farm, along with blacksmiths, mechanics, and laborers.

Durham's town farm was a real business operation. The town paid for dozens of repairs and implements in 1846 and 1847 such as an ox harrow, a plow, a cheese press, hay forks, a grindstone crank, and a hooping tub. Various horses and oxen were shoed by Rufus Willey.[37] Something about food and clothing can be learned from the receipt accounts, too. Along with entries for "tailoring" and "sewing" one finds specific references to linen thread, calico, "cassimere," "satinett," "frocking," twilled flannel, women's and boys' shoes, thick boots, and buttons.[38] Some of the clothes were made by townsmen. Others, it appears, were made by the paupers themselves, since these supplies were often bought in bulk.

Doubtless the paupers ate vegetables, fruits, animals, and dairy products from the farm. The food mentioned in this town farm account is of preserveable items, most of which were not likely to have been town farm products. Little & Co. was paid $2.56 for thirty-three pounds of coffee and $3.00 for one hundred pounds of sowns (oat porridge) and mackarel.[39] The paupers were also supplied with tea, corn, flour, beef, pork, salt, peas, oats, potatoes, molasses, and rice.[40]

Life on the farm had its small comforts too. Eight snuff boxes were purchased in 1845. Seven ounces of snuff were purchased in 1847. There are entries for tobacco and a pair of cards. The town paid 35 cents for a book for Alonzo Bickford in 1865. It appears that alcohol was a forbidden luxury. The account of 1861 says one pint of spirits was bought for the farm. Almost certainly this was for medicinal use only.[41] At the time, intemperance was considered to be the most common cause of pauperism.[42] Finally, medical care was provided by A. Bickford, who was paid $20.00 on May 19, 1846, "for services as physician at almshouse per agrt." Wistar's pills and balsam and "C. oil" (castor oil?) were purchased for the paupers.[43]

Town poor farms were run like businesses as well as correctional institutions; separate financial accounts were kept for them.

The yearly inventory and appraisal of property on Lee's poor farm includes a section on farm produce. The paupers probably had little leisure time, since they were kept busy producing items like hay, potatoes, turnips, cheese, soap, cider, beans, oats, barley, lard, and flour, to name a few.[44]

The population of the Lee poor farm did not grow; indeed, it declined slowly in the 1870s. This mirrored the area's general population decline (a similar situation occurred in Durham, as will be seen shortly). Tracing both the furniture inventory and the farm production record for Lee over the period 1859-1873, a small decline is noticeable. There were nine beds in 1859; by 1872 there were seven. More revealing is the decline from twenty-six milk pans in 1859 to seventeen in 1872, ten knives and forks to only two knives and forks, and eleven chairs to only three in 1872.[45] Perhaps there was some sharing of household utensils among the paupers. However, the decline in farm production almost certainly indicates a decline in the number of paupers working on the farm, barring the effects of climate and weather. For example, the poor farm produced twenty-six tons of hay in 1859; in 1872 it produced only five and a half. There were one hundred and twenty-eight bushels of corn in 1859; in 1872 there were only twenty-five. Forty pounds of butter were made in 1859 while only ten pounds were made thirteen years later.[46]

The most informative poor farm accounts for Durham are the annual reports of 1856 and 1859-1867. Like the poor farm in Lee, Durham's operation was run like a business as well as a house of correction: "with no moneys advanced by the town, this department has not only been self-sustaining for the term named [three years] but a source of income."[47] In Durham, a new administrative position was created in the 1850s, when the office of overseer of the poor was separated from that of keeper of the almshouse. The keeper actually lived on the farm and managed it, leaving the overseer of the poor free to perform other tasks such as community supervision.

Some of Durham's annual reports list farm production. Hay, butter, cheese, and potatoes were produced, as in Lee. Durham's poor farm was more engaged in raising and selling livestock than Lee's farm. The account of 1860, among others, lists many transactions involving steer, oxen, calves, cows, bulls, and heifers.[48] Durham's poor farm also made money by supplying labor for Durham townsmen. Sometimes paupers were hired from the farm to do specific tasks like butchering, drawing plank, or whitewashing. At other times, it looks as if they were hired just for general labor at $1 a day.[49] Unfortunately, there is not enough information available on Lee's poor farm operation to say whether any of its inmates were hired out as in Durham. In any case, it was the farm, not the pauper, who was paid.

The decline in the number of paupers maintained on Durham's poor farm resembles that of Lee's farm. Sometimes it is possible to determine the approximate number of paupers from the farm's list of itemized expenses. At other times the inventory lists the number of beds at the farm, as in Lee's records. The most helpful Durham accounts are for 1861 and 1865. Appraisers John Thompson and John H. Odiorne reported in 1861 that the average number of paupers for that year was twelve, and at the time there were eleven inmates.[50] The one and only available list of inmates of the Durham poor farm is located in the 1865 annual report. Susan Johnson, John Durgin, Alonzo Bickford, Mrs. Dame and child, Pamelia [sic] Smith, Samuel Dame, and Martha Short are the eight paupers listed.[51] The inventory declines from a high of twelve beds in 1861 to only eight beds in 1866.[52]

While Durham and Lee were committing paupers to their poor farms, Madbury continued to rely on "outdoor" relief. At no point in the available sources is there ever a reference to a poor farm in the town of Madbury. It is possible that a poor farm was proposed in Madbury sometime between 1827 and 1852, but the absence of available sources makes this impossible to determine. It is unlikely that Madbury would do so, however, because its resources were probably too few. In 1830 Madbury had 510 inhabitants; by 1850 the number was down to 483.[53] Too few paupers lived in Madbury to make a poor farm worthwhile, and a low tax base would have made it hard to raise enough money to acquire one. Instead, Madbury continued to rely mainly on "outdoor" relief. But poor relief was more complex in 1852 than it had been in 1827. From a cost of $79.34 in 1827, poor relief in Madbury jumped to $594.11 in 1852 (see Appendix, Table III).[54] The old "letting out" system described in Chapter II was prevalent in 1827. Poor children such as Nancy Allen were still being "bound out."[55] Except for some reimbursements to Rochester, Madbury's poor relief was confined within town borders.

The situation changed greatly over the next quarter of a century. Madbury residents still were paid by the town to maintain indigent citizens, but there was a new reliance on other towns and on the state of New Hampshire. Although the "letting out" system began to die out in the early nineteenth century, it did survive in some places in New Hampshire until the 1850s and later.[56] Most of the town paupers of Madbury in 1852 were boarded with fellow citizens at anywhere from $50 to $100 a year.[57] Since no mention is made of "letting out" expenses, it may be that this form of "outdoor" relief was changing. Perhaps the resemblance to an auction was disappearing.

Madbury seems to have relied on outside assistance for problem paupers. Ingals Burnham and Louisa Buzzell were sent to the Dover almshouse. Apparently Burnham was no problem, but Buzzell required a number of visits from doctors Jeremiah Horne, P.A. Stackpole, and A.G. Fenner. Medicine was also supplied to the unfortunate woman. The town finally was forced to rely on the state when Louisa Buzzell was taken to the New Hampshire Asylum for the Insane in Concord. She cost Madbury $63.71 for state aid alone.[58] Louisa Buzzell was a lunatic pauper. As reformers like Dorothea Dix observed, care for the insane was often crude and inadequate, if not actually cruel, in the nineteenth century. Those families who could not or would not care for a lunatic themselves left the burden upon the town. Like other infirm, sick, or crippled town charges, a lunatic was considered to be a pauper if he could not support himself and had no relatives able to do so. For instance, in 1846 the town of Lee voted for the selectmen to "take Oliver P. Wilson and carry him to the Town Farm and there chain him."[59] This passage sounds like a confirmation of the horrid conditions described by Dorothea Dix.

Louisa Buzzell was sent annually to the state insane asylum from 1852 through 1857.[60] The importance of the Buzzell case is that it illustrates a new development in poor relief: the beginnings of centralized administration of relief. It is true that the other poor of Madbury were maintained within the town or in Dover, but the fact that Madbury could and did rely on a state institution for a problem pauper shows that the days of independent administration of relief were numbered. As early as 1842, the New Hampshire legislature passed a law concerning insane paupers. The law stated that any insane town pauper might be sent by the overseers of the poor to the state asylum, to be maintained at town expense.[61] The state exerted its control when it declared that insane county paupers had to be sent to the state asylum and maintained at county expense.

Indeed, the question of whether or not a town was liable for the support of a pauper now assumed a position of importance. The old measure of "warning out" strangers was repealed in 1825.[62] With an increase in mobility came a threat to the old stable ways of life. More detailed laws were passed to protect New Hampshire towns from financial burdens incurred by nonresident paupers. A good example of this was a special provision made in 1831 for the burial costs of county paupers. The law stated that when a county pauper died, the town which had maintained him "shall cause such pauper to be decently buried." The bill for funeral and burial expenses was to be sent to the county treasurer, who would reimburse the town "in the same manner as is provided for the allowance and payment of claims on counties for the support and maintenance of paupers."[63] The conditions of settlement, described in Chapter II, were used to determine whether a pauper was an inhabitant or not. If not, he was considered to be a county pauper.

Provisions were also made to discourage the appearance of nonresident paupers. Fines were levied on anyone helping nonresident paupers come into the area. For example, the *Revised Statutes* of 1842 say in Chapter 67, "Of the Disposal and Support of County Paupers," that anyone conveying a pauper from another state into New Hampshire was liable to a $50 to $300 fine and six months in jail. If anyone attempted to bring a pauper from one county to another, he risked a $30 to $200 fine and a six-month prison sentence. Three years later, in 1845, anyone caught bringing in an out-of-state pauper was liable to paying a fine of $100 to $500, serving one year in jail, and assuming the costs to the town or county in New Hampshire for maintaining the pauper.[64] Such penalties were possibly directed at careless shipmasters who might inadvertently leave a town burdened with an impoverished passenger, labor contractors who were trying to find employees for the mills, or unscrupulous public authorities who might try to dump their own unwanted paupers on another locality.

Because careful distinctions were now being made between town and county paupers, the administration of poor relief in Durham, Lee, and Madbury was losing its strictly local character. Among the various entries for town poor, one finds the towns billing Strafford County for the maintenance of county paupers. On January 22, 1857, Madbury was paid $130.97 "for porpers" by the county. Lee received $318.44 for "County Paupers" in 1844. Durham was paid $421.00 in 1860 for maintaining county paupers on its town poor farm.[65] According to the available sources, none of the towns was in the position of paying Strafford County for maintaining town paupers before the Civil War. However, the construction of a county poor farm in 1866 and the subsequent disbandment of the town poor farms of Durham and Lee changed the picture, as will be seen in Chapter IV. Meanwhile, the towns paid their own poor bills for paupers within their borders or for charges incurred by their own paupers in neighboring towns. The only exception was the New Hampshire Asylum for the Insane. Madbury had to pay the state for the care of mad Louisa Buzzell in the 1850s. Durham had to pay the state for the care of Elizabeth Willey at the insane asylum in 1858 and 1859.[66]

The interference of county government in local poor relief was one aspect of the general growth of county power in New Hampshire. Early in the nineteenth century, the county government began to exercise an influence on some town affairs. The big change came in 1856, when the state legislature gave county commissioners authority to supervise all county affairs, roads, and the care of *town* paupers.[67] Such expansion of county power was partly due to popular dissatisfaction with the inadequacy of local governments. A more important impetus for county and state involvement was the centralizing role of the Civil War.[68] Financial strains and mobilization for military service were too much for local governments to handle; thus, state and county involvement in local affairs expanded noticeably in the 1860s.

Madbury had no town poor farm, so it continued to rely on "outdoor" relief. Durham and Lee acquired town poor farms in the 1830s. This did not mean that "outdoor" relief was dead. On the contrary, both Durham and Lee continued to maintain some paupers on "outdoor" relief. The annual reports for Durham and Lee have separate listings for paupers on the farm and paupers "off" or "away from" the farm.[69] Obviously the lunatics sent to the state asylum were in the second category. Some of the poor not on the farm required medical assistance. In 1856 Dr. A. Bickford of Durham was paid $19.17 for "medical attendance &c. on Moses Drew's son." In other cases, the poor received the usual "outdoor" type of relief. Lee spent $10.78 on wood, $16.00 on supplies, $1.00 in doctor's bills, and $3.50 for a coffin for John Leathers in 1845.[70] If a pauper incurred expenses in another town, he was also listed under the poor away from the farm. Nicholas and Jacob Willey of Durham were among the "poor not on the farm," because Newmarket billed Durham $13.25 for supplies furnished the pair.[71] Of the three towns, only Madbury appears to have continued to rely heavily on "outdoor" relief. Few of the paupers maintained off the farms of Durham and Lee were actually boarded with families as in the old days.

The significance of this is that paupers maintained off the poor farms of Durham and Lee were not likely to be completely destitute. Some were merely furnished supplies, while others received medical care. The poor off the farm were probably the borderline cases who had just enough resources to keep themselves from total poverty. It is quite likely these borderline paupers struggled to stay off the farm because they did not want to be associated with its inmates.

The small town of Madbury probably found it too costly to purchase or build a poor farm. There were around ten paupers each year who were maintained at Madbury's expense.[72] Approximately the same number of people were maintained in each of the poor farms of Durham and Lee until the 1860s. Madbury might have found it to be more economical to maintain paupers on "outdoor" relief and in other towns than to try the town farm system. The financial data for the town poor farm period in the three towns are quite sketchy.

Durham and Lee spent more money than Madbury on poor relief between the 1830s and 1870s. When Durham switched to "indoor" relief in 1834, it was paying around $300 to $500 a year in poor relief (see Appendix, Table I). This continued until at least 1843, when a gap appears in the data. From 1856 through 1867, when Durham sold its poor farm, the town spent thousands of dollars a year on poor relief. Most of the time it cost around $1200 to $1500 a year. As soon as the farm was sold in 1867, poor relief costs dropped precipitously to the $150 range and slowly rose thereafter.

Practically no financial information is available for Lee between 1845 and 1877. It is possible to determine that at the time Lee purchased its poor farm (1837), its poor relief costs were around $600 a year and rising (see Appendix, Table II). The purchase of the farm raised costs tremendously in 1838. This was followed by a tremendous drop, which in turn was followed by sharply rising costs until 1844, when costs had risen to around $880 a year. The next available figure is for 1878, when Lee sold its poor farm. Relief costs were now down to under $100 a year.

Madbury's records are so scanty between the 1830s and 1870s that no definite conclusion can be made about annual poor relief expenses. In 1827 costs had declined to under $100 a year. Nothing more is known until twenty-five years later, when costs had risen to the $600-a-year range (see Appendix, Table III). Thereafter poor relief costs declined tremendously, down to $150 a year by 1857. In 1870, when Madbury started to rely on the county poor farm, costs had risen to the $450 range.

While Durham and Lee switched to "indoor" relief, they ended up paying more than did Madbury, which stayed with "outdoor" relief at least until the 1870s. Even when one considers the costs of poor relief as a percentage of all annual town expenditures, this trend is evident. Madbury spent between 8% and 28% of its annual budget on poor relief during the studied time period, mainly staying around 20% (see Appendix, Table III). Durham's poor relief costs also stayed mainly at about 20% of the total annual budget, but they soared to over 50% in the early 1860s and fell to less than 5% at the end of the Civil War (see Appendix, Table I). As soon as the Durham farm was sold, the town's poor relief costs stayed at the very low level of under 5% for nearly a decade. In Lee, over time poor relief costs jumped from about 20% to nearly 45% of annual town expenditures (see Appendix, Table II). When its poor farm was disposed of in 1878, poor relief constituted a tiny 0.33% of the budget. But before the reader concludes that Durham and Lee engaged in a losing proposition while Madbury craftily managed to save money, two considerations should be borne in mind: the incompleteness of the original sources and the financial disruptions caused by the Civil War.

Since there are no available records on poor relief in Madbury during the 1860s, the effects of the Civil War on relief expenditures will have to be confined to Durham and Lee. The Civil War, like the Revolutionary War, interfered with the customary administration of poor relief. The difference was that the state government became far more involved in local poor relief than ever before.

Lee attempted to meet the increased expenses by itself. Starting on March 11, 1862, the town voted that the selectmen had power to disburse money to the soldiers' wives "as they think is needed."[73] This effort was inadequate to meet the burden, as Lee voted to raise money by taxation, and finally, to borrow money to pay the wives and families of volunteers in 1863.[74] It is impossible to determine whether the town was forced to rely on the state for aid.

Durham's expenses arising from the war started with enlistment bonuses and military supplies in 1861.[75] In 1862 Durham appealed to the state government. The families of forty-four volunteers received $2850.01 in state aid. These payments ranged from a low of $4 for the family of Alfred Stevenson to $132 for Charles W. Filbrick's family. Most of the soldiers' families received about $60 each year from the state.[76] These families continued to receive similar quantities of state aid until May 1, 1865. Most of this information is contained in the annual reports for 1863 through 1866; the rest is in an untitled handwritten book in *Durham Town Records: Accounts & Business 1700-1866*. Durham sold its town poor farm shortly after the Civil War. State aid to volunteers' families was stopped, and poor relief expenses dropped rapidly.

Both the Civil War and the construction of a state insane asylum changed the character of poor relief in Durham, Lee, and Madbury. Along with a limited degree of state involvement, the three towns had to adjust to the participation of the county government in poor relief administration. As will be seen in Chapter IV, closer cooperation with the county in regard to poor relief was not always desired by the town governments.

The days of the town poor farm in Durham and Lee were numbered. The Strafford County Almshouse was constructed in Dover in 1866. As fewer paupers were committed to the town institutions, the ability of the Durham and Lee poor farms to pay for themselves by farm production was diminished. The three towns felt economic and political pressures turning them toward a closer involvement with the county for the administration of poor relief in the post-Civil War era.

NOTES TO CHAPTER III

1. *Sixth Census or Enumeration of the Inhabitants of the United States, as Corrected at the Department of State, 1840* (Washington, 1841), 33 and J.D.B. DeBow, superintendent of the U.S. Census, *The Seventh Census of the United States: 1850* (Washington, 1853), 21.

2. Joseph C.G. Kennedy, *Population of the United States in 1860: Compiled from the Original Returns of the Eighth Census* (Washington, 1864), 304-305.

Poor Relief In Durham, Lee, and Madbury 61

3. *Sixth Census*, 25; Kennedy, *Population of United States in 1860*, 309, and Robert P. Porter, superintendent, *Compendium of the Eleventh Census: 1890, Part I -- Population* (Washington, 1892), 275.

4. *Sixth Census*, 25 and DeBow, *Seventh Census*, 21.

5. Francis A. Walker, *A Compendium of the Ninth Census (June 1, 1870) Compiled Pursuant to a Concurrent Resolution of Congress, and Under the Direction of the Secretary of the Interior* (Washington, 1872), 531-535.

6. *Ibid.*, 531-535.

7. *Collier's Encyclopedia*, 1977 ed., "The United States of America."

8. DeBow, *Seventh Census*, 2; Kennedy, *Population of the United States in 1860*, 304-305; and Walker, *Ninth Census*, 3.

9. Leah H. Feder, *Unemployment Relief in Periods of Depression* (New York, 1936), 327.

10. Nellie P. George, *Old Newmarket New Hampshire* (Exeter, N.H., 1932), 62 and 83.

11. A.E.G. Nye, comp., *Dover, New Hampshire, Its History and Industries Issued as an Illustrated Souvenir in Commemoration of the Twenty-fifth Anniversary of Foster's Daily Democrat* (Dover, 1898), 50.

12. *Ibid.*, 47.

13. William D. Knapp, *Somersworth An Historical Sketch* (1894), 55.

14. Franklin McDuffee, *History of the Town of Rochester New Hampshire, From 1722 to 1890*, v. II., (Manchester, N.H., 1892), 502.

15. Frank B. Sanborn, *New Hampshire: An Epitome of Popular Government* (Boston, 1904), 240-241.

16. *Copy of the Town Records of the Town of Durham, N.H. 1732-*

1841, 4 Original. October 21, 1820 - March 29, 1832, 122-123.

17. *Town of Durham, 1732-1841*, 4 March 1832 - Dec. 1841, 204.

18. *Ibid.*, 206.

19. New Hampshire. Strafford County, *Register of Deeds*, 156/179-180, Dover Court House.

20. *Town of Durham, 1732-1841*, 4 March 1832 - Dec. 1841, 229.

21. *Ibid.*, 229.

22. *Ibid.*, 235.

23. *Ibid.*, 245.

24. *Town Records 1825-1851*, 65.

25. *Ibid.*, 74 and 108.

26. *Ibid.*, 196.

27. New Hampshire. Strafford County, *Register of Deeds*, 175/274, Dover Court House.

28. Cited in Sophonisba P. Breckinridge, *Public Welfare Administration in the United States*, 2nd. ed., (Chicago, 1938), 33.

29. David J. Rothman, *The Discovery of the Asylum* (Boston, 1971), 196.

30. *Town of Durham, 1732-1841*, 4 March 1832 - Dec. 1841, 248.

31. Edwin C. Bean, ed., *Laws of New Hampshire*, IX (Concord, N.H., 1921), 754.

32. *Town of Durham, 1732-1841*, 4 March 1832 - Dec. 1841, 248.

33. Bean, *Laws of New Hampshire*, IX, 754.

34. *Town Records 1825-1851*, 145.

35. Rothman, *Discovery of Asylum*, 193.

36. *Town Records 1825-1851*, 145.

37. *Receipts & Expenditures of the Town of Durham, for the Year Ending Feb. 20, 1847*, 5.

38. *Ibid.*, 4-7.

39. *Ibid.*, 3.

40. *Ibid.*, 3-6.

41. *Receipts and Expenditures and Report of the Superintending School Committee of the Town of Durham, for the Year Ending March 1st., 1861* (Dover, N.H., 1861), 1.

42. Breckinridge, *Public Welfare Administration*, 37.

43. *Receipts & Expenditures, 1847*, 6.

44. *Town Farm: Yearly Inventory and Appraisal of Property on the Farm 1859-1873*.

45. *Ibid.*

46. *Ibid.*

47. *Receipts and Expenditures and Report of the Superintending School Committee of the Town of Durham, for the Year Ending March 1, 1864* (Lynn, Mass., 1864), 12.

48. *Receipts and Expenditures of the Town of Durham, For the Year Ending March 1st., 1860* (Dover, N.H., 1860), 13-15.

49. *Receipts and Expenditures, 1861*, 14.

50. *Ibid.*, 17.

51. *Receipts and Expenditures and Report of the Superintending School Committee of the Town of Durham, for the Year Ending March 1, 1865* (Dover, N.H., 1865), 25.

52. *Receipts and Expenditures, 1861,* 17 and *Receipts and Expenditures of the Town of Durham, For the Year Ending February 22, 1866* (Dover, N.H., 1866), 27.

53. *Fifth Census, or Enumeration of the Inhabitants of the United States in 1830* (Washington, 1832), 10-11 and DeBow, *Seventh Census,* 21.

54. *Town Book. Treasurer's Record 1755-1826* and *Town of Madbury Annual Report 1852,* 5.

55. *Treasurer's Record 1755-1826.*

56. Benjamin J. Klebaner, "Pauper Auctions: The 'New England Method' of Poor Relief," *Essex Institute Historical Collections* 91 (1955), 204.

57. *Madbury Report 1852,* 3-4.

58. *Ibid.,* 4-5.

59. *Town Records 1825-1851,* 256.

60. *Madbury Annual Report, 1852,* 4-5; *Madbury Report, 1854,* 2-3; and *Town of Madbury Expense Account 1856-1858,* 2, 5, 7, 13, and 16; and *Receipts & Expenditures of the Town of Madbury, for the Year Ending March 1, 1855* (Dover, N.H., 1855), 2.

61. *The Revised Statutes of the State of New Hampshire; Passed December 23, 1842* (Concord, N.H., 1843), 56.

62. Bean, ed., *Laws of New Hampshire,* X (Concord, N.H., 1922), 236.

63. *Ibid.,* 236.

64. *Revised Statutes 1842,* 140-141 and *Laws of the State of New*

Hampshire; from November Session, 1842, to June Session, 1847, Inclusive (Concord, N.H., 1847), 237.

65. *Madbury Expense Account 1856-1858*, 8; *Receipts and Expenditures in the Town of Lee, for the Year 1844*, 1 in *Miscellaneous Town Papers, 1801-1845*; and *Receipts and Expenditures, 1860*, 15.

66. *Receipts and Expenditures of the Town of Durham, For the Year Ending March 1st., 1859* (Dover, N.H., 1859), 4-5 and *Receipts and Expenditures, 1860*, 15.

67. Leon W. Anderson, *200 Years of New Hampshire Counties 1771-1971*, 3.

68. Morton Keller, *Affairs of State: Public Life in Late Nineteenth Century America* (Cambridge, Mass., 1977), 115.

69. See *Lee Receipts and Expenditures, 1844*, 2 and *Report of the Overseer of the Poor: Also of the Selectmen & Treasurer, of the Town of Durham, for the Year Ending March 1, 1856* (Dover, N.H., 1856), 6-7 as examples.

70. *Lee Receipts and Expenditures, 1845*, 1 in *Miscellaneous Town Papers, 1801-1845*.

71. *Receipts and Expenditures, 1859*, 5.

72. See *Madbury Report 1852*, etc.

73. *Town Records 1862-1872*, 6.

74. *Ibid.*, 52-53.

75. *Receipts and Expenditures and Report of the Superintending School Committee of the Town of Durham, for the Year Ending March 1st., 1862* (Dover, N.H., 1862), 10-11.

76. *Receipts and Expenditures and Report of the Superintending School Committee of the Town of Durham, for the Year Ending March 1, 1863* (Dover, N.H., 1863), 6-7.

CHAPTER IV

Post-Civil War Poor Relief

County and state involvement in local poor relief administration increased gradually after the Civil War. Already the county had assumed a role in pre-Civil War days with provisions for county paupers and county poor farms. By 1866, Strafford County had its own almshouse in Dover. Morton Keller says that there was a cycle of growth and decline in state and local government: "state taxation and expenditure sharply increased in the Civil War decade from three to six times in most northern commonwealths. Heavier spending went hand in hand with a dramatic rise in the sheer scale of state legislation."[1] This was more evident in some states than others. Massachusetts was a leader in the centralizing process -- the early state poor farms in the first state civil service commission in 1885.[2]

The most noticeable growth in county and state power in New Hampshire took place between 1828 and the 1870s. In 1828, counties were empowered to construct county poor farms.[3] The New Hampshire Asylum for the Insane was opened in 1838 and the State Reform School was started in 1851.[4] Once the Civil War ceased to be an impetus, state government involvement in the whole country, as well as in New Hampshire, shrank. Localism, laissez-faire, and hostility to centralized government slowed down the process of state and county involvement in poor relief in the post-Civil War era.[5] Nevertheless, poor relief in Durham, Lee, and Madbury had been affected by this process; it was no longer an exclusive town province.

There was some outspoken resistance to the centralizing trend; even after Durham and Lee disbanded their town farms, the three towns continued to maintain most of their paupers without county or state assistance. Durham, Lee, and Madbury were affected by outside developments: 1) the construction of the Strafford County Almshouse in 1866, 2) the passage of various state laws respecting poor relief administration, and 3) a large increase in the number of wandering paupers.

This chapter will cover the post-war era through 1891. The latter date has been chosen for several reasons. First, United States census reports concerning poverty are extant only for 1850 through 1890. Also, the basic pattern of local New Hampshire poor relief was in place by 1891 and would remain essentially unchanged until the 1930s despite the efforts of Progressive reformers. Finally, 1891 was the twenty-fifth anniversary of the Strafford County Almshouse. Durham and Lee disposed of their town farms in 1867 and 1878, respectively, and thus by 1891 it is possible to see how much of an effect the county institution had on local poor relief over a twenty-five year period. Certainly after a quarter-century the county institution was firmly in place and an established factor in local poor relief administration.

Since the 1820s, New Hampshire towns had been billing county governments for the maintenance of county paupers. Status as a county pauper was determined by the settlement law of 1796, which remained basically unchanged throughout the entire nineteenth century (see Chapter II). Essentially, a county pauper was a pauper who had no legal settlement. Those county paupers not confined to the county farm were maintained by the towns in which they resided. The county was billed for such paupers' maintenance by the towns concerned. According to John Scales, Strafford County historian, towns overcharged counties for boarding county paupers. To correct this problem, in 1866 the state legislature gave New Hampshire counties the authority to purchase or construct their own almshouses to avoid paying the towns' exorbitant charges.[6] Actually, the counties had had authority to build almshouses since 1828, but at that time there had been no mention of overcharging by the towns.

Strafford County Commissioners Joseph F. Lawrence of Lee, Andrew Rollins of Rollinsford, and Uriah Wiggin of Dover purchased the 165-acre John Trickey farm in Dover for $9500 in 1866. They also bought the adjoining Timothy Snell farm for $6000 and some additional land, which made for 283 acres in all. A new brick house was constructed on the spot for $16,000, and Mr. and Mrs.

Cornelius E. Caswell were the first superintendents of the county poor farm.[7] Durham was not at all pleased with this development.

Durham voters roundly condemned the county farm at the town meeting of March 13, 1866. The records state, "Resolved, that it is the deliberate judgment of the people of the Town of Durham that the proposition to establish a county farm for the support of the poor of the County of Strafford is founded on erroneous principles; is injudicious and uncalled for; and would add largely to the expenses of the County, without improving the condition of the Poor; and that our Representatives be instructed to oppose it in all its stages of progress."[8]

Lee's response to the new county institution was more ambiguous; if anything, the voters of Lee were mostly in favor of it. The Lee town records for 1862-1872 indicate that the town was anxious to get rid of its own poor farm. Along with the decline in farm production and number of paupers actually living on the farm, the buildings required a great deal of maintenance.[9] Fifteen of Lee's citizens saw fit to sign a petition asking the selectmen and voters to sell the poor farm and disburse the money from its sale among the town's voters. This petition was made "in consideration of the decision to procure a County Poor-farm." A decision on the matter was "indefinitely postponed" because it was illegal to distribute the money from the sale among Lee's voters.[10] Whether any of Lee's citizens were as irate over the county farm as those in Durham or not, Lee continued to rely on its poor farm for a dozen more years.

Madbury sent Francis Cole to be maintained for a year at the county farm in 1869, so if there was any opposition to the institution in that town, it was short-lived.[11] Madbury, like Durham and Lee, was increasingly drawn into closer cooperation with the county government by state laws affecting poor relief. Since 1791 counties had been liable for the support of paupers who had no settlement status. As time went on, more explicit instructions were given in the New Hampshire laws as to which paupers were to be maintained by towns and which by counties.

The first law concerned exclusively with "county" as opposed to "town" paupers is found in the *Revised Statutes* of 1842. Chapter 67, "Of the Disposal and Support of County Paupers," was passed as a measure to help New Hampshire towns cope with an increasingly mobile number of paupers. Here county paupers are defined as those paupers not having settlement status. Overseers of the poor are instructed to bill the county for the maintenance or burial of nonresident paupers within one year. This law also lists the penalties for conveying nonresident paupers into the county or state from elsewhere. Shipmasters had to post a $200 bond for each out-of-state passenger and securities worth three years' poor relief. If they did not do so, shipmasters could be fined $200 per passenger and spend a year in jail. If a person conveyed a pauper from one county to another, he risked six months in jail and a fine ranging from $30 to $200.[12]

A major extension of county power into local poor relief was the passage of "An Act In Relation to the Powers and Duties of County Commissioners" in 1860. County commissioners now had authority to contract for the support of county paupers with "any party or parties" or to send such paupers to the county poor farm. "No town shall be entitled to receive compensation for the support of such paupers after neglect or refusal to comply with such order or regulation notice thereof having been given to the overseers of such town."[13] Despite its peremptory tone, this law was designed to help towns cope with wandering paupers. It was a practical measure too; towns would be able to afford to care for poor strangers temporarily while the county found someone to do so on a more permanent basis. Such an agreement between the county and a town was mutually beneficial, especially if the county poor farm was too small to house all the county paupers or was nonexistent. As of 1860, Strafford County still did not have a county institution. Durham, Lee, and Madbury all boarded county paupers at county expense.

From the 1850s on, New Hampshire lawmakers were increasingly concerned about wandering paupers. Fines for transporting paupers from one county to another were raised and jail sentences lengthened. Starting in 1855, provisions were made to keep foreign paupers and criminals out of New Hampshire.[14] Renewed attention was given to the conditions necessary for establishing settlement. In 1866 New Hampshire lawmakers sought to solve the problem of mobile paupers by appealing directly to New Hampshire voters. A state law required town selectmen to insert the following article into town warrants: "Is it expedient to abolish pauper settlements [the establishment of resident status] in towns and throw the entire support of paupers upon counties?"[15]

The people of Lee voted decisively against this measure: seventy-seven "nays" to nine "yeas."[16] Despite the fact that Durham voted thirty-five to twenty-seven in favor of the abolition of pauper settlements, the town decided that it should at least maintain its own poor.[17] Pauper settlements were not abolished in the rest of New Hampshire either. New Hampshire towns succeeded in maintaining some degree of autonomy in poor relief administration. The problem of wandering paupers was not really solved.

Post-Civil War records on poor relief have many references to "transients," "tramps," and travellers." Lee spent $23.00 on tramps in 1879, who were probably a product of the big depression on 1873-1879.[18] There are other references to tramps in later years, too. Starting in 1868, Durham had to care for many travellers or transients. In 1878 alone, David Stevens billed the town $91.20 for "keeping 254 transients."[19] Madbury seems to have been singularly free from the wandering poor in the post-Civil War period, or at least free from paying for them, anyhow. This is quite a contrast to the late eighteenth century, when Madbury was "warning out" a greater number of poor strangers and undesirables than either Durham or Lee. For the post-Civil War period, there is only one reference to wandering paupers in Madbury: in 1870 Benjamin F. Hayes received $3 "for helping a poor person on his way."[20]

Despite Durham's opposition, the Strafford County Almshouse was built in 1866; the influence of other towns within the county, and of Dover, the county seat, was too much. In late 1866, Durham voted to sell its town farm and the personal property on it. In the spring of 1867, the town sold the farm for $7200.00 and personal property on it for $1440.80, making a total of $8640.80.[21] Daniel Chesley bought 126 acres of land from the town, most of which was part of the poor farm, for $5625.00, on March 29, 1867. George W. Palmer purchased the remaining 23 acres of the former town farm with buildings for $1575.00 on March 30.[22]

Even though the town farm was now gone, Durham's voters insisted on maintaining their own poor in 1867, rather than sending them to the county facility.[23] Perhaps Durham's experience with its own institution had at least temporarily convinced the voters that sending the town poor to the county institution would not be an improvement. Aside from paying Joseph C. Bartlett of Durham $12 for "carrying paupers to County Farm" in 1868, there is no mention of the county institution in the reports of the overseer of the poor until 1872.[24] The paupers transported by Mr. Bartlett were probably transients or county paupers. In 1872, for the first time, Durham actually paid Strafford County to maintain paupers; the town had held out for five years before giving in.

Lee debated selling its poor farm in 1866, the year the county farm was opened in Dover. Proposals were made to sell it by auctioning it off, and to use the money from the sale to pay the town's debts.[25] The petition urging the town to sell its poor farm and take advantage of the new county farm has already been described. Despite the sentiment in favor of selling the town farm, Lee voted not to sell it.

Over the next eleven years Lee still debated the question. At one point, the town even considered leasing out the farm.[26] Finally, on December 8, 1877, Lee voted to sell the personal property on the farm and to advertise the auction of the farm itself in March, 1878.[27] Daniel Smith bought Lee's former poor farm for $1970 on March 11, 1878.[28] Poor relief accounts in the town's annual reports after 1878 provide no information as to whether Lee maintained any paupers at the county farm. For some years, the only listing is "paupers" and the cost of their relief. There is no mention of the county farm in the Lee records which do have itemized expenses.

Madbury never had to worry about disbanding a town farm, and the few records available indicate that it rarely used the county farm. One possible reason Lee and Madbury rarely used the county farm, if at all, was the expense. Starting in 1866, the county charged $1.50 per week for pauper maintenance.[29] On the other hand, instead of having to pay, the towns would be adequately compensated by Strafford County for boarding county paupers. A law of 1873 states that county commissioners might contract with town selectmen to support county paupers for such reasons as "long residence or local associations" at up to $1.50 per week.[30] Throughout the 1870s and 1880s, all three towns were paid varying amounts to maintain county paupers.

The annual reports of the county commissioners list paupers maintained at the county farm from Durham, Lee, and Madbury. A crucial distinction is made by the county commissioners in the report of 1867: Madbury was the only town sending town paupers to the farm; all the rest (those from Durham and Lee included) were county paupers.[31] This is probably the reason why Durham and Lee's annual town reports do not mention these paupers.

Along with a greatly increased level of county involvement, local poor relief was also affected by the appearance of state institutions. New Hampshire followed the national trend with the establishment of state institutions for certain classes of paupers. The state insane asylum had been in operation since 1838, giving towns the option of sending their insane paupers away for proper care.[32] The care of indigent children and juvenile delinquents also received attention: the State Reform School was established in 1851 (it became the State Industrial School in 1881), and the New Hampshire Orphans' Home was opened in Franklin in 1871.[33] In 1862 the state resolved to send deaf and dumb paupers to the Hartford, Connecticut, state asylum. Blind and partially blind indigent people could be sent to the Boston, Massachusetts, state institution.[34] Just as Connecticut and Massachusetts cooperated with New Hampshire to care for the indigent deaf, dumb, and blind, so did New Hampshire cooperate with Rhode Island, which sent lunatics to the New Hampshire state asylum.[35]

Massachusetts led the way in state supervision of poor relief when it established the country's first board of state charities in 1863.[36] Other states followed slowly, while New Hampshire did not have its own state board for another three decades.

The state boards were not exclusively concerned with poor relief, but rather with the whole range of public dependency, from prisons to insane asylums to dependent children. At the same time, poor relief came under the scrutiny of the Charity Organization Societies. Their purpose was to ensure better management of private charity efforts. They also affected the administration of public relief. In 1889, the National Conference of Charities and Corrections counted seventy-five organized member societies throughout America.[37] The private charitable orphans' homes in the state are mentioned in the conference records, but it is uncertain if they were among the member societies.[38]

The significance of the state boards and the Charity Organization Societies is that, on a national level, poor relief administration was becoming centralized. Now accurate statistics on pauperism were being kept. Reformers pressured state and county governments to disburse poor relief more efficiently and honestly.

New Hampshire did not have a state board of charities until thirty years after its neighbor in Massachusetts. In the eyes of late-nineteenth-century reformers, New Hampshire was a backward state when it came to poor relief. The Committee on Reports from States of the 1889 Conference of Charities and Corrections commented on this. The committee deplored the unorganized and incomplete status of the data on poverty in New Hampshire. For instance, it said, "The county reports do not separate these insane paupers from ordinary paupers in their accounts."[39]

The level of state and county interference in the poor relief administration of Durham, Lee, and Madbury was not high compared to that in other states such as Massachusetts. If anything, state assistance was something of a convenience for the three towns, judging from their records. They could send a lunatic pauper to the state asylum and so avoid the trouble of caring for a potentially dangerous person in their midst. They could send a juvenile delinquent to a state institution for correction. Only a few children were sent to such a place. Joseph H. and Lewis P. Caverly of Madbury were maintained for a year at the State Reform School in 1869-1870 for $163.14. So too was Margaret A. Kidder of Madbury for $44.56.[40] Annie Ring of Durham was boarded at the State Industrial School for $29.14 in 1891.[41]

Apparently only Durham had to resort to the New Hampshire Asylum in the post-war period. The town sent William K. Chesley to the asylum for seven years (1872-1878) and then again in 1881. Mrs. Nancy A. Frost was committed to the asylum for one year, in 1884.[42] The county took care of an insane tramp in 1886. Doctor S.H. Greene attended him for $1.50 and J. Dennison transported the wretched man to the county farm for $3.00.[43]

The state assumed a more assertive role in town affairs when it came to aiding impoverished Civil War veterans. In 1885, the legislature insisted that towns and counties must shoulder the financial burden of veteran aid. It was forbidden to send poor veterans and their families to almshouses. A state Soldiers' Home was incorporated in 1878.[44] Generally, "outdoor" relief was prescribed at the veteran's own home "or such place other than a town or county almshouse."[45] Even though such veterans were dependent on public aid, they were not to be classified as paupers. The state imposed a $500 fine on any town which did so. Separate accounts from those for regular poor relief had to be kept for needy veterans.[46] It was probably because these poor veterans had served honorably that the state authorities insisted they not be classified as "paupers." Yet probably only a small proportion of these veterans, mainly those who had been seriously wounded, could claim in 1885 that their dependent condition was due to their service in the Civil War.

Indeed, "An Act In Relation to Aid Furnished to Indigent Soldiers and Providing for Entrance to the Soldiers' Home in Certain Cases" set down rather strict conditions for those veterans who would apply for relief in 1891. As with town paupers, there was a settlement requirement: the veteran must have been a town or county resident for at least three years. Next, he had to present a certificate "of a reputable physician, resident in the county in which he lives, that he is incapacitated to peform manual labor," probably the most important condition for relief. The veteran also had to rely on his federal pension for self-support; he was forbidden to sell articles supplied him by the town or county, and he was forbidden to trade them in exchange for liquor. The temperance movement was strong in 1891. He was forbidden to share received aid with anyone other than his immediate family. If he disobeyed these provisions, he was to be sent to the town or county almshouse with the rest of the paupers.[47]

Eight "needy soldiers" of Durham were provided with "supplies" worth $1293.17 in 1887. This was nearly four times the $355.01 spent on town paupers. Adding these two figures together, poor relief was the most expensive item on Durham's budget for 1887, other than state and county taxes.[48] It made up 17.56% of the budget, the largest figure since 1864 (see Appendix, Table I). Again in 1890 and 1891, when the town was obliged to furnish aid to the veterans, poor relief constituted between 10% and 15% of the budget, a level not seen since 1864 (see Appendix, Table I).

Aid to needy veterans was a lighter burden for Lee and Madbury. The only record for Lee is in the 1891 annual report, when the town spent $170.44 on "soldiers' aid."[49] The total amount spent on poor relief was $432.04, which constituted 10.65% of the annual expenditures for 1891, a fairly high but by no means unusual figure for Lee since the early 1880s (see Appendix, Table II). Madbury spent only $126.50 on soldiers' aid in 1891 and $197.74 on the rest of its paupers.[50] The total $324.24 spent on poor relief in Madbury in 1891 was only 6.95% of the budget, a figure which had not varied much since 1870 (see Appendix, Table III).

Of the three towns, Durham was by far the most seriously burdened by state laws concerning poor veterans. It had a larger population than either Lee or Madbury, and it had sent a larger number of men to fight in the Civil War (see the figures for state aid to soldiers' families during the war in Chapter III). In the town meeting of 1866, Durham voters expressed dismay at the county's interference. How did they feel about the large burden imposed on them by the state regarding poor veterans? The records are silent. Perhaps it would have seemed unpatriotic to complain in this case.

Unlike some of the eighteenth- and early nineteenth-century records, the poor relief accounts for Durham, Lee, and Madbury of the almshouse period are not very informative as to the identity of the paupers. Thus it is very difficult to compare the local poor farm and county farm populations with those of New Hampshire or of the whole United States.

Judging from the available sources, Durham, Lee, and Madbury did not follow the national trend in poor relief in 1880. The census statistics report there were far more paupers maintained in almshouses in the United States than were maintained by "outdoor" relief. In that year, there were 66,203 almshouse paupers in America and only 21,595 "outdoor" paupers. The trend was less pronounced but still similar for New Hampshire as a whole: 1198 almshouse and 839 "outdoor" paupers.[51] In contrast, Durham, Lee, and Madbury relied much more on "outdoor" relief in 1880 than on "indoor." Ten paupers are mentioned by name in the Durham account for 1880. Of these, only one, Isabella Hurd, was maintained at the county farm in Dover. All of the rest were boarded in citizens' homes (presumably not by the old "letting out" system) or received aid in their own homes.[52] One of the nine "indoor" paupers was William K. Chesley, who was temporarily maintained out of the state insane asylum. He had spent most of the 1870s there and was to return to state "indoor" relief three years later.

On the other hand, the annual report of the county commissioners mentions four paupers from Durham by name, including Isabella Hurd.[53] It is not stated here whether one, some, or all were town or county paupers. If one considers the preponderance of town paupers maintained on "outdoor" relief, it seems likely these were county rather than town poor.

Neither the Lee annual report of 1879 nor the one of 1881 enlightens us beyond the fact that Lee spent under $100 a year on poor relief. It is almost certain that Lee relied on "outdoor" relief in 1880 like Durham, for three reasons. First, the town poor farm was no longer in use, having been auctioned off in 1878. Second, there is no mention of payments to Strafford County other than tax. Third, the annual report of 1882 lists "outdoor" relief expenses.

Once again, the county records help out where the town records are silent. In 1880, there were eight paupers from Lee maintained at the county farm.[54] Eight was an unusually high number for Lee; normally, Lee sent only a couple or so paupers each year to the county farm. Since the town records make no mention of payments to Strafford County (other than tax), and they do list payments from the county to the town for "county paupers," an interesting situation is suggested.

Perhaps the county paid towns to maintain nonresident (*i.e.* county) paupers who were associated with those particular towns (relatives or previous employment there may have been the reason for this association). Using the money received from the county, the towns boarded at least some of these county paupers at the county institution. It was probably left to the towns to decide whether it was more convenient (or cheaper) to maintain county paupers at home or at the county farm.

Madbury expended only $103.50 on poor relief in 1880. It was all "outdoor" relief: John and Ellen Church were boarded at the home of Ira A. Locke, J. Frank Seavey & Co. was paid for clothing John Church, and James J. Griffin got $1.50 for keeping tramps that year.[55] The one pauper maintained at the county farm in 1880 was sixty-five-year-old Winthrop Burnham. This pauper was still at the farm in 1891.[56]

The tables on physical condition and form of disability of almshouse paupers in New Hampshire and the United States for 1880 list fourteen status possibilities. Once again, the incompleteness of the records of Durham, Lee, and Madbury, and the fact that the three towns relied overwhelmingly on "outdoor" relief in 1880, make a real comparison impossible.

In both the national and state tables, insanity is the leading form of disability for almshouse paupers. 252 out of the 1198 almshouse inmates of New Hampshire were insane.[57] As has been seen, all three towns had insane paupers at one point; however, none of them were in an almshouse in 1880. 229 children were in New Hampshire almshouses in 1880, along with 156 idiots. The state's almshouses contained lesser numbers of intemperate, sick, lame and crippled, epileptic, and blind paupers.[58] Perhaps the Strafford County almshouse was as bad as reformers of the day said almshouses were.

One modern historian, David J. Rothman, writes that the almshouse population "itself became compelling evidence of the need for institutionalization. Its corridors were filled with first and second generation immigrants along with the broken, aged, diseased, crippled, and dissolute."[59] A New Hampshire historian of the early twentieth century reports a much brighter picture of the almshouse. Writing about Strafford County, John Scales says, "But as a general thing the poor on these town farms were well cared for, had plenty to eat and drink, perhaps too much cider at times, and plenty of clothing to keep them warm in winter."[60]

By 1890 the almshouse population of New Hampshire had declined slightly, to 1143.[61] The census report for 1890 is the only one which provides a breakdown of this population by county. The Strafford County almshouse had 191 paupers that year. Only the Hillsboro County almshouse, with 273 inmates, was larger.[62] Not one of the Strafford County almshouse paupers in 1890 came from Durham, Lee, or Madbury.[63] It looks as if the three towns relied on the county farm sporadically and for only a few paupers at a time.

Chapter III described the noticeable population decline experienced by all three towns throughout the nineteenth century. With fewer paupers to maintain and no poor farms of their own in 1890, it may have seemed more economical to take care of the town poor themselves. Of course, the state laws of 1885, 1889, and 1891 concerning poor veterans added a significant financial burden to the towns' poor bills.

Durham's annual poor relief expenses dropped sharply in 1868, after the town farm was sold (see Appendix, Table I). Over the next decade, these expenses rose from around $90 a year to over $450, and settled back down to the $100-per-year range. Such expenses were normally under 5% of the entire yearly expenditure.

Durham's expenses gradually increased in the 1880s. In 1887 poor relief expenses shot up to $1648.18, or 17.56% of the annual budget, because of the poor veterans. After a temporary drop in 1888, poor relief expenses continued their upward trend, so that by 1891 Durham was spending $2043.24 a year on poor relief (15.65% of the total annual town expenses).

Little information is available on Lee's financial burden until six years after it sold its poor farm in 1878. At that point Lee's poor relief expenses were small ($77.36), making up 8.21% of the annual budget (see Appendix, Table II). Toward the end of the 1880s, Lee's poor relief expenses rose to the $300-and-more-per-year range, with expenses rising to $641.04, or 21.36% of the budget, in 1889. In 1891 the figure was back down to $259.35 (10.65%).

Finally, Madbury's poor relief figures are very incomplete until 1880. Expenditures remained remarkably steady for this final decade, unlike in Durham and Lee. Madbury spent between $100 and $300 a year, which varied between 2.68% and 7.64% of the total annual town expenses (see Appendix, Table III). This was both a lower and more consistent range of expenditures than that experienced by either Durham or Lee.

Two important developments characterized poor relief

administration in Durham, Lee, and Madbury after the Civil War. County and state participation in local poor relief was increased substantially while the almshouse system of relief was largely abandoned. The county relied on the towns to maintain more county paupers than ever before (for payment). At the same time, the towns had a new opportunity to send their paupers to the county poor farm in Dover; few of them resorted to it. Along with the state insane asylum, the state reform or industrial school was also made available for special types of town paupers. Apparently there were no deaf, dumb, or blind paupers in the three towns. Laws passed in the 1860s made it possible for them to turn such paupers over to the state, which would place them in special institutions in Boston or Hartford, Connecticut.

The state exerted its growing control near the end of the period covered, when it passed legislation concerning poor veterans. Not only did the state force towns to care for their veterans, but it outlined the conditions for relief (terms of settlement and what the recipient was permitted to do with the money or supplies provided). Poor relief in Durham, Lee, and Madbury was increasingly affected by county and state decisions, following the national trend toward centralized administration.

The towns' reversion to "outdoor" relief followed the trend for New Hampshire, but not for the nation. In 1880 there were 66,203 almshouse paupers in the whole country; by 1890 there were 73,045. In 1880 New Hampshire had 1198 almshouse paupers; in 1890 there were 1143.[64] The state's population as a whole was growing: 346,991 inhabitants in 1880 and 376,530 in 1890.[65]

Almshouses were the targets of social critics throughout the late nineteenth century. Such criticism was not new, but it received a greater degree of publicity than formerly. Along with the usual expressions of horror at the shocking conditions within, reformers held up the almshouse as an example of political corruption. "The poorhouse has been too often, though not always, the cheapest of the spoils of politics for plunder only," declared Homer Folks, a Progressive reformer, in 1894.[66]

It is unlikely that Durham, Lee, or Madbury professed any such reason for their lack of enthusiasm for the Strafford County poor farm. Compared to states like Massachusetts, New York, Pennsylvania, and Ohio, New Hampshire was rather backward in poor relief administration.[67] The most likely reason the three towns maintained most of their poor on "outdoor" relief after selling their poor farms was that it was the most economical method in their circumstances.

Possibly, the Congregational Church played a role in local relief. Rather than submit to outside authority, small town congregations may have regarded local poor relief as something they could handle independently. The Church could partially substitute for the charitable organizations which were active in aiding the poor in other parts of the country. It is also possible that some local sentiment for autonomous poor relief administration prevailed; Durham had expressed dismay and opposition to the idea of a county farm in 1866.

By 1891 poor relief as practiced in Durham, Lee, and Madbury had assumed the form it was to keep until the 1930s. The towns could rely on state institutions for special paupers now. They could use the county facility as well, but as has been seen, they were not overly enthusiastic to do so. In some ways the old methods were still being used. The towns relied on themselves to a large degree and "outdoor" relief was still practiced. Paupers were not being "let out" at auction anymore, but New Hampshire overseers of the poor still had authority to "bind out" poor children and adult paupers to local citizens who would take them in. It was not until 1937 that "binding out" paupers was finally abolished.[68]

NOTES TO CHAPTER IV

1. Morton Keller, *Affairs of State Public Life in Late Nineteenth Century America* (Cambridge, Mass., 1977), 110.

2. *Ibid.*, 322.

3. Leon W. Anderson, *200 Years of New Hampshire Counties 1771-1971*, 8.

4. *Index to the Laws of New Hampshire Recorded in the Office of the Secretary of State 1679-1883* (Manchester, N.H., 1886), 27 and 519.

5. Keller, *Affairs of State*, 115.

6. John Scales, *History of Strafford County New Hampshire and Representative Citizens* (Chicago, 1914), 52.

7. *Ibid.*, 53.

8. *Durham Town Records, 6 1865-94*, 32.

9. See for example *Town Records 1862-1872*, 66.

10. *Ibid.*, 258.

11. *Annual Report of the Receipts and Expenditures of the Town of Madbury, For the Year Ending March 1st., 1870* (Dover, N.H., 1870), 4.

12. *The Revised Statutes of the State of New Hampshire: Passed December 23, 1842* (Concord, N.H., 1843), 140-141.

13. *Laws of the State of New Hampshire, Passed June Session, 1860* (Concord, N.H., 1860) in *Laws of New Hampshire 1853-60* (bound pamphlets), 2253-2254.

14. *Laws of the State of New Hampshire, Passed June Session, 1855* (Concord, N.H., 1855) in *Laws of New Hampshire 1853-60* (bound pamphlets), 1610.

15. *Session Laws of New Hampshire, 1861-66*, 3277.

16. *Town Records 1862-1872*, 301.

17. *Durham, 6 1865-94*, 46 and 53.

18. *Annual Report of the Selectmen and Treasurer and Superintendent of Public Schools, of the Town of Lee, N.H. for the Year Ending Mar. 1, 1879* (Newmarket, N.H., 1879), 8.

19. *Annual Report of the Selectmen and Treasurer and Superintending School Committee, of the Town of Durham for the Year Ending March 1, 1878* (Dover, N.H., 1878), 6.

20. *Annual Report, Madbury 1870*, 4.

21. *Durham, 6 1865-94*, 40-41 and *Report of the Selectmen's Accounts and the Superintending School Committee of the Town of Durham, N.H., From Feb. 25, 1867, to March 6, 1868* (Dover, N.H., 1868), 4.

22. New Hampshire. Strafford County, *Register of Deeds*, 241/161-164, Dover Court House.

23. *Durham, 6 1865-94*, 53.

24. *Durham, Report of 1867-1868*, 9 and *Annual Report of the Selectmen and Treasurer, Overseer of the Poor, and Superintending School Committee, of the Town of Durham, for the Year Ending March 1, 1872* (Dover, N.H., 1872), 7.

25. *Town Records 1862-1872*, 246.

26. *Town Records 1872-1896*, 133.

27. *Ibid.*, 152.

28. New Hampshire. Strafford County, *Register of Deeds*, 264/31, Dover Court House.

29. Scales, *Strafford County*, 53.

30. *Laws of the State of New Hampshire, Passed June Session, 1873* (Concord, N.H., 1873), 171.

31. Joseph F. Lawrence, Andrew Rollins, and Uriah Wiggin, *Commissioners' Report for Strafford County* (in bound pamphlets at Dover Public Library), (1867), 8.

32. *Index to Laws 1679-1883*, 27.

33. *Ibid.*, 519, 516, and 400.

34. *Session Laws 1861-66*, 2639 and 2643-2644.

35. Sophonisba P. Breckinridge, *Public Welfare Administration in*

the United States, 2nd. ed., (Chicago, 1938), 529.

36.   *Ibid.*, 248.

37.   Oscar C. McCulloch, "Report of the Standing Committee," *Proceedings of the National Conference of Charities and Correction at the Sixteenth Annual Session Held in San Francisco, Cal., September 11-18, 1889* (Boston, 1889), 10.

38.   J.P. Bancroft, "Reports from States. Report of the Committee. New Hampshire," *Proceedings 1889*, 155.

39.   *Ibid.*, 155.

40.   *Annual Report, Madbury 1870*, 3.

41.   *Annual Report of the Selectmen, Treasurer and Overseer of the Town Poor of the Town of Durham, for the Year Ending March 1, 1891* (Dover, N.H., 1891), 6.

42.   See *Annual Reports of Durham, 1872-1878*, and *1881* and *Annual Report of the Selectmen and Treasurer and Superintending School Committee, of the Town of Durham, for the Year Ending March 1, 1884* (Dover, N.H., 1884), 6.

43.   *Annual Report of the Selectmen and Treasurer and Board of Education, of the Town of Durham, for the Year Ending March 1, 1886* (Dover, N.H., 1886), 8-9.

44.   *Index to Laws 1679-1883*, 509.

45.   *Laws of the State of New Hampshire, Passed June Session, 1885* (Manchester, N.H., 1885), 251.

46.   *Laws of the State of New Hampshire, Passed June Session, 1889* (Manchester, N.H., 1889), 96-97.

47.   *Laws of the State of New Hampshire, Passed January Session, 1891*, 333.

48.   *Annual Report of the Selectmen, Treasurer, Board of Education, of*

the Town of Durham, for the Year Ending Mar. 1, 1887 (Dover, N.H., 1887), 5 and 9.

49. *Annual Report, Lee 1891*, 6.

50. *Annual Report of the Selectmen and Treasurer and School Board of the Town of Madbury for the Year Ending March 1st., 1891* (Dover, N.H., 1891), 4.

51. Frederick H. Wines, *Report on the Defective, Dependent, and Delinquent Classes of the Population of the United States, As Returned at the Tenth Census (June 1, 1880)* (Washington, 1888), 447-448.

52. *Annual Report of the Selectmen and Treasurer and Superintending School Committee of the Town of Durham, for the Year Ending March 1, 1880* (Dover, N.H., 1880), 4.

53. George Lyman, Cyrus Littlefield, and Samuel A. Seavey, *Annual Report of the Commissioners of the County of Strafford, and Reports of the Superintendent of the County Farm, Treasurer, Jailer, Physician, Solicitor, Sheriff, and Clerk of the Courts, For the Year Ending March 30, 1880* (Dover, N.H., 1880), 12.

54. *Ibid.*, 13.

55. *Annual Report of the Selectmen, Treasurer, and Superintending School Committee of the Town of Madbury, For the Year Ending March 1st., 1880* (Dover, N.H., 1880), 4.

56. Lyman, Littlefield, and Seavey, *Annual Report, Strafford County 1880*, 13 and Charles E. Demeritt, *Annual Report of the Commissioners of the County of Strafford, Together With the Reports of the Superintendent of the County Farm, Treasurer, Jailer, Physician, Solicitor, Sheriff, and Clerk of Courts, For the Year Ending April 30, 1891* (Dover, N.H., 1891), 31.

57. Wines, *Defective, Dependent, and Delinquent Classes at the Tenth Census*, 470-471.

58. *Ibid.*, 470-471.

59. David J. Rothman, *The Discovery of the Asylum* (Boston, 1971), 290.

60. Scales, *Strafford County*, 52.

61. Frederick H. Wines, *Report on Crime, Pauperism, and Benevolence in the United States at the Eleventh Census: 1890. Part II. General Tables* (Washington, 1895), 651.

62. *Ibid.*, 682.

63. See *Annual Report, Madbury 1891*, 4; *Annual Report, Durham 1891*, 13-14; and *Annual Report of the Selectmen and Treasurer and School Board of the Town of Lee, for the Year Ending Mar. 1, 1891* (Dover, N.H., 1891), 6.

64. Wines, *Defective, Dependent, and Delinquent Classes at the Tenth Census*, 470-471 and Wines, *Report on Crime, Pauperism and Benevolence at the Eleventh Census*, 651.

65. *Statistics of the Population of the United States at the Tenth Census (June 1, 1880)*, v. 1, (Washington, 1883), 71 and Robert P. Porter, superintendent, *Compendium of the Eleventh Census: 1890. Part I -- Population* (Washington, 1892), 2.

66. Homer Folks, "The Removal of Children from Almshouses," *Proceedings, 1894*, 120.

67. See Bancroft, "Reports from States," *Proceedings, 1889*, 152-156.

68. The New Hampshire Historical Records Survey Project Division of Professional and Service Projects. Works Projects Administration. (Sponsored by U.N.H.), *Town Government in New Hampshire* (Manchester, N.H., 1940), 72.

CHAPTER V

Conclusion

The three towns of Durham, Lee, and Madbury, New Hampshire, generally followed national trends in poor relief administration during the eighteenth and nineteenth centuries. Along with most of the United States, Durham and Lee made the change from "outdoor" to "indoor" relief in the 1830s. As county and state governments became more involved in local affairs throughout the nation in the 1860s, so did they in New Hampshire. In only one respect was poor relief in the three towns significantly different from the national picture: they had no local secular charity organizations active in the late nineteenth century. It is true that most charitable activity took place in urban regions, whereas Durham, Lee, and Madbury were small farming towns. But it is also true that New Hampshire was considered to be a backward state in poor relief administration during the late nineteenth century.

The size of the towns was a significant factor in the poor relief developments described in this paper. In the eighteenth century, Durham and Lee were fairly large towns with populations of over a thousand residents; Madbury was fairly small, having around six hundred. Thus, none of the towns was a city, and it was up to the individual town governments to devise methods of supporting their own poor. Relying on both English precedents and Yankee practicality, Durham, Lee, and Madbury engaged in "outdoor" relief. Poor strangers were "warned out" (but not always successfully, as the presence of Mariam Clemmons in Lee attests). Where feasible, the poor were maintained in their own residences with supplies or medical care furnished at town expense. Most often, town paupers were "let out" to other town residents (normally for a one-year term) to labor for their keep. "Letting out" made sense in the three prosperous agricultural communities.

Illness and injury added significantly to the costs of local "outdoor" relief. Many of the paupers required medical care, usually for unspecified illnesses. Some had injuries, such as Eli Demeritt of Durham "since he Broak his arm."[1] Unwed mothers with illegitimate children cost the towns money as well.

It appears that impaired health or injury by themselves were sometimes the cause of a person's poverty in Durham, Lee, and Madbury. Perhaps the pauper's life was so hard and uncomfortable that his health was ruined further, requiring medical attention. This suggestion is fairly unlikely, since there are a number of contracts and indentures for "let out" paupers, specifying the mutual obligations between the pauper and the person boarding him. The frequency of medical expenses in the old poor relief accounts might be partially explained by the fact that many of the paupers were old. Rural medicine of the eighteenth century was probably inadequate to cure sickly old paupers already weakened by a hard primitive existence.

It is impossible to say from the evidence available whether or not "outdoor" relief via "binding out" poor children and "letting out" or "bidding off" adults was cruel in practice. Benjamin J. Klebaner claims that this form of relief placed a premium on "meanness and avarice," could break up pauper families, and was a system designed to exploit the pauper for all the labor in him.[2] "Outdoor" relief may well have been ungenerous in the three towns, but there are at least three reasons for believing it was not as bad here as Klebaner describes.

First, the amount of money bid on paupers varied from one year to another. There are a number of explanations for this: the state of the economy, the resources of those bidding, and the potential value of each pauper's labor. But since nearly all the paupers of these three towns were "let out" for some money, they were worth something and could not be considered simply as slaves working for nothing. The money spent on them was supposed to go for the paupers' maintenance.

Secondly, the contracts or indentures extant explicitly state the obligations of both paupers and bidders. Selectmen and overseers of the poor were supposed to ensure that both sides kept to the agreements.

A third reason is speculative: since there are no complaints in the records, "outdoor" relief as practiced in Durham, Lee, and Madbury was reasonably satisfactory. It is true enough that the powerless members of any society are usually not heard. But some of the paupers here were probably literate. In addition, the small sizes of Durham, Lee, and Madbury meant that most of the town poor were relatives of other citizens. In a number of cases, the town poor and higher officers like selectmen share the same family name. The significance of this is that if conditions were very bad, someone would complain at a town meeting out of pity if nothing else. It was not until the 1820s that paupers were actively feared and disliked.

Practically none of the original sources consulted, however, gives expression to the new attitude towards poverty and paupers. Since nearly all of them consist of dry financial data or terse accounts of town meetings, it is not easy to find confirmation of the negative attitude toward paupers described by Bremner and other historians. There are indirect clues, however: 1) the fact that Durham and Lee did implement "indoor" relief in the 1830s, 2) the designation of the poor farms as houses of correction, and 3) the treatment of insane Oliver P. Wilson of Lee.

There are both economic and political reasons for the appearance of "indoor" relief in Durham and Lee. Thanks to outside developments, the local economy entered a long period of decline and change in the nineteenth century. The economic foundation of ship building and farming was seriously weakened by Westward migration and technical innovations. As Americans moved West, they began to farm the rich new lands of New York, Ohio, the Midwest, and so on. As new transportation lines were established, and railroads, steamboats, and canals appeared, the New England farmer fell into trouble. More, better, and cheaper produce from the West undercut New Hampshire's agricultural base. Transportation lines between the great Eastern port cities and the rich hinterland bypassed this area, cutting into the ship-building industry too.

While Durham, Lee, and Madbury were faced with a declining agricultural economy, they were also faced with another nineteenth century development: industrialization. Early in the century, textile and woolen mills were established in the nearby towns of Newmarket, Dover, Somersworth, and Rochester, among others. Nineteenth century census reports indicate that while Durham, Lee, and Madbury suffered a population decline, these mill towns expanded. Some of the people moving in to work in the mills must have come from the declining rural areas.

The importance of these major economic developments is that they provide a partial explanation for the change from "outdoor" to "indoor" relief. Boarding out paupers to work for their keep may not have seemed so worthwhile by the 1830s. The paupers' economic value as farm laborers may have been declining (recall the dramatic decrease between 1819 and 1833 in the amount bid by Durham bidders). Perhaps as more townsmen became wage earners they found it less worthwhile to have a pauper on the premises, since there was not enough work for the pauper to do. Also, as Americans became more mobile, there was a new concern over wandering paupers. One way to deal with the problem was to confine them to one location (in almshouses) where they could be cared for and supervised. Why did Durham and Lee turn to the almshouse? Economic changes were not reason enough.

The town leaders of Durham and Lee must have been at least partially influenced by social reformers of the day. Durham's poor farm opened in 1834 and Lee's opened in 1838; this was the heyday of "indoor" relief. As David J. Rothman points out, America turned to "indoor" relief because of the new perception of poverty as unnatural and alarming. Reformers believed that poverty was a curable condition; a condition mainly due to moral shortcomings in the poor person's character. It seems unlikely that citizens of Durham and Lee would not also subscribe to these theoretical reasons for confining paupers to an almshouse, as well as subscribing to the economic reasons illustrated above.

One piece of evidence which seems to confirm this is the designation of the Durham poor farm as a house of correction in 1834, the year it was opened. A house of correction's very purpose was to "correct" deviants. Virtually all undesirable persons, ranging from "rogues" to "common night walkers" to "pilferers," were condemned to the house of correction along with the paupers. Lee too seems to have considered its poor farm to be a house of correction. Two paupers found the conditions intolerable and ran away. Several years later, a lunatic pauper named Oliver P. Wilson was conveyed to the farm and chained. These actions seem to indicate that yes, indeed, local citizens had theoretical as well as practical reasons for implementing "indoor" relief in the 1830s.

Was "indoor" relief a success? For Durham and Lee, the answer would have to be not much. "Indoor" relief was not a total failure, but there were too many forces working against it. Some citizens opposed it from the very beginning, and it took several years in both towns to get the proposal for an almshouse approved. Probably due to economic constraints, neither Durham nor Lee constructed a new building for their almshouses; both purchased rundown old farms instead. Extensive repairs were necessary before moving the poor in.

Certainly neither poor farm succeeded in rehabilitating the poor. Reality was working against the dream of nineteenth-century reformers all over America: "indoor" relief just did not "cure" paupers. This was partly due to human nature. Several other factors contributed to the almshouses' lack of success. First, no real provision for pauper classification was made -- thus, all sorts of unfortunates and misfits were mixed within the almshouse and, in most cases, neglected. Madbury and Durham took advantage of the New Hampshire Asylum for the Insane, which relieved this problem somewhat. Also, there is no indication that political chicanery was a problem in the towns covered here, but nationally it attracted attention. While corrupt politicians benefited, the almshouses and their inmates suffered as necessary funds were diverted. Administrative procedures tend to solidify in most bureaucracies, and this was the case with American "indoor" relief. Twenty or thirty years after the almshouse system became widespread, its faults became visible. New methods of poor relief were still in the future.

A declining population may also have been a factor in the lack of success of "indoor" relief in Durham and Lee. Starting in the 1840s, Strafford County entered into a long period of decline and stagnation. While the county itself grew slowly over the rest of the nineteenth century, the populations of Durham, Lee, and Madbury continued to decline. Several reasons for this population decline have been suggested, including a declining local economy as ship building and farming went under, and emigration from the three towns to the West, the cities, and to other New Hampshire towns where the textile mills were flourishing.

Just as the towns' populations declined, so did their number of poor farm inmates. With fewer paupers to work on the poor farm, "indoor" relief may have been too expensive to be worthwhile. Poor relief expenditures went down significantly in both Durham and Lee after they sold off their town farms (see Appendix, Tables II and III). It was probably too expensive to run the poor farms for a small and declining number of paupers for several reasons. In the first place, the farm buildings of both towns required lots of maintenance. Secondly, both towns paid superintendents to live on and manage the farms. As the number of paupers decreased, these fixed costs did not. The most important effect of the declining population was that with fewer paupers to work on the poor farms, the ability of the poor farms to pay for themselves was seriously impaired.

From the beginning, productive employment had been one of the goals of "indoor" relief. Ideally, the town's poor farm would pay for itself. Sometimes this actually happened. In 1864 E. Thompson, overseer of the poor of Durham, proudly reported that Durham's institution was actually a moneymaking operation.

The declining poor farm population meant that farm production was in decline as well. This was true for both Durham and Lee. Thus both Durham in the late 1860s and Lee in the late 1870s were faced with unproductive poor farms and high fixed costs. All of these factors sounded the death knell for the poor farms of Durham and Lee. But this did not mean the "indoor" relief was dead.

As the census reports of 1880 and 1890 show, "indoor" relief continued to be the most common method of handling the poor throughout America. It is no surprise to learn that the Strafford County Almshouse was established in 1866, several decades after the rage for "indoor" relief had swept across the country. By this time, "indoor" relief was well-established, in spite of its unsuccessful record. An interesting point is that neither Madbury, nor Lee, nor Durham ever relied heavily on the county poor farm in the post-Civil War era. Three possible reasons explain this state of affairs: 1) local resentment of the trend toward centralized poor relief, 2) the cheapness to the towns of caring for their own paupers, and 3) the experiences of Durham and Lee with their own poor farms made them unenthusiastic about county "indoor" relief.

Local resentment was strongly expressed in Durham. Its citizens complained about the county poor farm, tried to stop it, and apparently sent no town paupers there for the first six years of its existence. Even when Durham began sending paupers to the county poor farm, it sent only a very small number. Lee never complained much, but neither did it praise county involvement. An important point is that Lee did not send a single town pauper to the Strafford County poor farm in the late nineteenth century, according to the available sources. It looks as if Madbury never complained, but that town, too, entrusted very few paupers to county care.

The most likely reason for Madbury's minimal response to county aid was that it was more economical to take care of its town poor by itself than to rely on the county farm. It was a village of under four hundred people by 1890, which meant that the few paupers requiring assistance could be boarded easily with town citizens. This saved time, effort, and money: Madbury's poor relief expenses were small in the post-Civil War period. They stayed between 3% and 7% of annual town expenditures, a very low figure for all three towns, during the entire period from 1732 to 1891.

Poor relief costs were higher and more erratic in the towns of Lee and Durham for the post-war period. It is important to note that these costs dropped greatly in both towns as soon as they sold their poor farms. In the case of Durham, which sold its poor farm in 1867, the sudden drop in poor relief expenditures may have been partially related to the fact that Civil War expenses had recently ended too. However, the Civil War cannot be used as an explanation for the sudden decline in Lee's poor relief expenditures, since that town's poor farm was sold later, in 1878. It is certainly possible that, based on their experience, town authorities decided that "outdoor" relief was cheaper than sending town paupers to the county almshouse. Their experience might also have informed them of the futility of "indoor" relief.

If Durham and Lee saw fit to disband their poor farms, why would they regard the county poor farm as any better? To be sure, the facility was a large, modern, brick building surrounded by acres of farmland, but the method of relief was unchanged. Several reasons have already been suggested for the failure of "indoor" relief in the United States. Town officials in Durham and Lee must have become acquainted with some of the failings of the poor farm system over the several decades it was practiced there.

Circumstances and decisions of the late nineteenth century in Durham, Lee, and Madbury resulted in what looks like a reversion in poor relief methods. While much of America was seeing increased county and state involvement in local poor relief, these three New Hampshire towns were apparently closing their doors to new developments. There are no records of either private or state charity in the poor relief accounts of late nineteenth-century Durham, Lee, and Madbury. In other parts of the country, this was a major new development. On the other hand, most of this charitable involvement took place in urban areas. New Hampshire as a whole was growing moderately in the final decades of the nineteenth century, but the three towns under investigation were losing inhabitants.

New Hampshire was considered a backward state in poor

relief administration compared to other states. Yet Durham, Lee, and Madbury were permanently affected by the developments in poor relief administration of the nineteenth century. They did indeed rely almost entirely on "outdoor" relief after Durham and Lee disbanded their town poor farms. Most town paupers were boarded with private citizens as of old, but with one important difference: paupers were no longer "let out" or "bid off" by auction. Instead, the overseer of the poor made financial arrangements with willing citizens for housing, feeding, and clothing town paupers. Probably the paupers were expected to contribute some labor for their upkeep, but this is never mentioned in the records of this later time, in contrast to those of the pre-almshouse era. Farming still went on here, but by the late nineteenth century textiles and manufacturing had largely taken over. Thus, the value of town paupers as farm laborers was much less than it had been previously, which meant that there was very little incentive for people to make bids to board such paupers as in the old days.

Another major difference between "outdoor" relief in the three towns in the post-Civil War era and that of the pre-almshouse days was the level of county and state involvement. All three towns were paid by Strafford County to maintain county paupers. Such paupers had not even existed in the old days. Such people used to be "warned out." By paying Durham, Lee, and Madbury to maintain county paupers, the state and county governments had found a partial solution to the problem of increasing numbers of wandering paupers. The towns also now had the option of sending some of their paupers to various state institutions, not to mention the county poor farm in Dover.

War brought the state government into local poor relief. For a brief period during the Revolution, the state government was petitioned (usually with success) by wounded ex-soldiers and widows of soldiers for state aid. The state contributed large sums of money for aid to soldiers' families during the Civil War. Twenty years later, Durham, Lee, and Madbury were still haunted by the war as the state legislature began enacting a series of laws requiring New Hampshire towns to maintain certain veterans at town expense. As noted, this could be quite costly. The state also specified which veterans were eligible and the conditions by which the recipient was to abide.

Poor relief in Durham, Lee, and Madbury, New Hampshire, followed most of the national developments described in Chapter I.

It was only in the late nineteenth century that local poor relief began to lag far behind the national trend. The manner in which the three towns took care of their poor citizens in 1891 remained essentially unchanged for the next four decades.

Every state, county, and town in America is unique in some way. The changes in methods of poor relief over nearly a hundred and sixty years in these three towns largely confirm what other historians have said about early American poor relief. It is hoped that this thesis has helped to illuminate an aspect of New Hampshire social history relevant to the problems of today. Just as the English Poor Law of 1601 influenced "outdoor" relief, and both of these, in turn, influenced "indoor" relief of the nineteenth century, so too some of the attitudes and practices of the past can help inform us on the problems of poor relief administration of the present day.

The controversy over public welfare is one such problem; as in the past, there is widespread hostility and resentment toward welfare recipients, who are viewed by many of New Hampshire's citizens as unworthy and lazy. Another related problem carried over from the past concerns the funding of public institutions ("indoor" relief) such as the state insane asylums in Concord and Laconia and the county rest home in Dover, a modern successor to the county poor farm. Funding is frequently difficult to find and there are periodic complaints about inadequate treatment for the inmates.

This investigation into poor relief of the past also reveals something of the present-day character of Durham, Lee, and Madbury. Most of the paupers, town officials, and citizens boarding the paupers, as written in the old records, have names which are still found in the area today. Some names are found in local families residing in the three towns; others are found in the names of roads. Local cemeteries and family graveyards are full of stones marked with these names as well. The Durham poor farm no longer stands on the right-hand side of Route 108, heading toward Dover; in its place stands a modern brick building which houses the New Hampshire Medical Foundation. The former Lee poor farm is now a family-run dairy farm on Wednesday Hill Road.

NOTES TO CHAPTER V

1. *Town Book. Treasurer's Record 1755-1826.*

2. Benjamin J. Klebaner, "Pauper Auctions: The 'New England Method' of Poor Relief," *Essex Historical Collections* 91 (1955), 196-199.

APPENDIX

APPENDIX

TABLE I

Poor Relief Expenditures
Durham 1751-1891

Year	Total Annual Town Expenditure (N)	Poor Relief Expenditure	Poor Relief Expenditure as % of Total (N)
1751	£101 17s 1.5d	£28 6s 5d	28.12%
1753	£436 12s	£119 6s 7d	27.35%
1754	£795 12s 5d	£66 7s 6d	8.37%
1755	£936 17s 4d	£92 5s 9d	9.86%
1756	£1118 17s	£87	7.77%
1757	£1495 8s 9d	£146 1s 3d	9.77%
1758	£2005 15s 10d	£141 8s 9d	7.06%
1759	£2391 13s 8d	£203 11s	8.52%
1760	£2278 8s 1d	£292 17s	12.88%
1761	£3014 10s 1d	£371 1s	12.31%
1762	£2556 16s 3d	£369 9s 7d	14.45%
1763	£2872 17s	£299 13s 6d	10.44%
1764	£1513 13s 3d	£467 3s 6d	30.86%

TABLE I continued

Year	Total Annual Town Expenditure (N)	Poor Relief Expenditure	Poor Relief Expenditure as % of Total (N)
1766	£82 16s 8d	£41 13s 6d	50.51%
1767	£156 4s 5d	£105 7s	67.53%
1768	£201 5s 11d	£80 9s 10d	40.10%
1769	£185 10s 6d	£36 10s 6d	19.83%
1770	£198 2s 10d	£33 2d	16.65%
1771	£212 2s 11d	£59 5s 9d	28.01%
1772	£199 8s 5d	£61 12s 9d	31.07%
1773	£246 11s 2d	£51 4s 7d	20.80%
1774	£173 4s 6d	£53 18s 1d	31.44%
1775	£75 1s 7d	£39 16s 4d	53.72%
1776	£191 14s 1d	£15 12s 11d	8.33%
1777	£1174 17s 4d	£266 6s 10d	22.68%
1778	£1532 8s 11d	£626 3s 7d	40.86%
1779	£8236 7s	£1715 12s 5d	20.83%
1780	£38,941 2s 6d	£11,162 19s 9d	28.67%
1782	£876 12s 10d	£155 14s 8d	17.81%
1798		$484.50	

TABLE I continued

Year	Total Annual Town Expenditure (N)	Poor Relief Expenditure	Poor Relief Expenditure as % of Total (N)
1801	$1019.80	$409.73	41.48%
1802	$1093.20	$458.34	41.92%
1803	$1404.76	$645.38	45.95%
1804	$1591.43	$284.66	17.71%
1805	$1451.71	$334.88	23.08%
1806	$3591.01	$1704.28	47.76%
1808	$2613.00	$650.00	24.04%
1809		$650.00	
1819		$995.00	
1820		$849.00	
1821		$774.00	
1822	$2317.81	$760.00	32.71%
1823	$2319.81	$462.00	10.56%
1824	$2437.47	$429.00	10.76%
1825	$2205.42	$445.00	20.13%
1826	$2041.92	$428.00	20.96%
1827	$2171.41	$475.00	21.87%

TABLE I continued

Year	Total Annual Town Expenditure (N)	Poor Relief Expenditure	Poor Relief Expenditure as % of Total (N)
1828	$2246.38	$500.00	22.26%
1829	$2536.38	$572.00	22.55%
1830	$2721.38	$488.00	17.93%
1831	$2089.66	$436.00	20.86%
1832	$2221.66	$500.00	22.50%
1833	$2197.12	$470.00	13.65%
1834	$2475.00	$401.93	16.24%
1835	$2752.43	$300.00	10.89%
1836	$2192.43	$350.00	15.96%
1837	$2092.05	$350.00	16.73%
1838	$2175.00	$350.00	16.09%
1839	$2177.00	$500.00	22.97%
1840	$2249.67	$450.00	20.00%
1841	$2211.74	$400.00	18.09%
1842	$2126.47	$400.00	18.81%
1843	$2522.88	$300.00	11.89%
1844	$2279.81	$400.00	17.55%

TABLE I continued

Year	Total Annual Town Expenditure (N)	Poor Relief Expenditure	Poor Relief Expenditure as % of Total (N)
1856	$4051.25	$1264.43	31.21%
1859	$3925.32	$1817.01	46.29%
1860	$8363.74	$4058.62	48.53%
1861	$5922.02	$3230.64	54.55%
1862	$5062.56	$1300.63	25.69%
1863	$5253.69	$1415.79	26.95%
1864	$6810.92	$1210.71	17.78%
1865	$35,319.41	$1075.83	3.00%
1866	$12,441.18	$1231.46	12.02%
1867	$14,047.95	$1231.46	8.77%
1868	$15,303.45	$102.48	0.67%
1869	$14,065.86	$117.19	0.83%
1870	$14,132.86	$84.65	0.60%
1871	$11,989.15	$161.97	1.35%
1872	$14,210.25	$266.76	1.88%
1873	$13,879.15	$187.17	1.35%
1874	$11,857.09	$330.97	2.79%

TABLE I continued

Year	Total Annual Town Expenditure (N)	Poor Relief Expenditure	Poor Relief Expenditure as % of Total (N)
1875	$14,009.56	$387.73	2.77%
1876	$9,165.00	$460.31	5.02%
1877	$7371.64	$542.73	7.37%
1878	$9262.09	$358.43	3.87%
1879	$6667.52	$138.25	2.07%
1880	$6459.55	$248.38	3.85%
1881	$8307.31	$399.56	4.81%
1882	$7493.72	$420.87	5.62%
1883	$7453.91	$449.79	6.03%
1884	$9939.64	$436.98	4.40%
1885	$8322.07	$198.03	2.38%
1886	$7770.61	$526.34	6.77%
1887	$9386.78	$1648.18	17.56%
1888	$9316.90	$292.06	3.13%
1889	$9951.43	$1491.68	14.99%
1890	$17,494.91	$1770.05	10.13%
1891	$13,057.73	$2043.24	15.65%

Sources:

"Contracts Respecting the Poor of Durham From April 1798," *Records on Paupers and Wharfs, 1798-1806.*

Copy of the Town Records of the Town of Durham, N.H. 1732-1841.

Durham, N.H., *Annual Report* (title varies) *1845/6-1891/2.*

Durham Town Records vol. 5: 1842-1864.

Town of Durham Accounts 1751-1782.

APPENDIX

TABLE II

Poor Relief Expenditures
Lee 1801-1891

Year	Total Annual Town Expenditure (N)	Poor Relief Expenditure	Poor Relief Expenditure as % of Total (N)
1801	$1196.54	$115.40	9.64%
1802	$681.88	$220.47	32.33%
1803	$1250.73	$175.66	14.04%
1804	$1117.57	$119.86	10.73%
1805	$1495.17	$79.44	5.30%
1806	$1680.10	$207.25	12.30%
1807	$1760.02	$432.30	24.56%
1808	$1476.34	$193.28	13.09%
1809	$1181.59	$135.84	10.65%
1810	$1085.50	$165.73	15.27%
1811	$1189.08	$288.96	24.30%
1812	$1252.55	$170.62	13.62%
1813	$2100.17	$173.52	8.26%

TABLE II continued

Year	Total Annual Town Expenditure (N)	Poor Relief Expenditure	Poor Relief Expenditure as % of Total (N)
1814	$1692.41	$218.80	12.93%
1815	$1344.03	$282.74	21.04%
1816	$1155.66	$268.45	23.23%
1817	$2031.48	$447.09	22.01%
1818	$2405.52	$296.48	12.32%
1819	$1993.70	$473.75	23.76%
1820	$1704.97	$455.50	26.72%
1821	$3490.92	$623.40	17.86%
1822	$4781.30	$270.00	5.65%
1823	$1493.78	$105.00	7.03%
1824	$1736.18	$232.00	13.36%
1825	$756.74		
1826	$1642.73	$349.97	21.30%
1827	$2856.61	$397.44	13.91%
1828	$2403.78	$376.67	15.67%
1829	$4713.84	$418.27	8.87%
1830	$4347.12	$528.07	12.15%

TABLE II continued

Year	Total Annual Town Expenditure (N)	Poor Relief Expenditure	Poor Relief Expenditure as % of Total (N)
1831	$3146.21	$567.67	18.04%
1832	$2562.66	$522.19	20.38%
1833	$2182.15	$434.37	19.91%
1834	$2120.76	$752.29	35.47%
1835	$6246.93	$495.36	7.93%
1836	$2818.27	$561.21	19.91%
1837	$2478.09	$503.46	20.32%
1838	$13,328.36	$3086.23	23.16%
1839	$6689.67	$277.03	4.14%
1840	$1645.45	$47.00	2.86%
1841	$1811.30	$270.72	14.95%
1842	$6700.71	$501.42	7.48%
1843	$1864.59	$372.69	19.99%
1844	$2000.06	$878.65	43.93%
1878	$6968.03	$23.25	0.33%
1879	$8029.92	$49.52	0.61%
1881	$9740.65	$98.97	1.02%

TABLE II continued

Year	Total Annual Town Expenditure (N)	Poor Relief Expenditure	Poor Relief Expenditure as % of Total (N)
1882		$112.11	
1883	$7596.29		
1884	$942.09	$77.36	8.21%
1885	$2821.71	$48.00	1.70%
1886	$1674.30	$47.72	2.85%
1887	$6174.76	$137.65	2.23%
1888	$3214.59	$360.49	11.21%
1889	$3000.96	$641.04	21.36%
1890	$6306.61	$434.04	6.85%
1891	$2434.94	$259.35	10.65%

Sources:

Annual Reports (title varies) *1844, 1878-1879, and 1881-1891*.

Payment Book 1809-1825.

Record of Payments and Receipts: Daybook 1802-09 v. I. and *1825-1842 v. III.*

APPENDIX

TABLE III

Poor Relief Expenditures
Madbury 1755-1891

Year	Total Annual Town Expenditure (N)	Poor Relief Expenditure	Poor Relief Expenditure as % of Total (N)
1755	£390 13s 11d		
1756	£573 6s 6d	£56 11s	9.92%
1757	£835 11s	£209 17s 4d	23.17%
1759	£1874 2s 4d	£196 1s 4d	10.46%
1760	£3510 19s 5d	£142 11s	4.10%
1761	£1596 4s	£178	11.15%
1762	£2166 6s 3d	£185 3s	8.55%
1763	£2084 10s 4d	£170 16s 6d	8.22%
1764	£2267 8s 9d	£102 10s	4.50%
1765	£697 10s 2d	£234 17s 4d	33.70%
1766	£38 19s 1d	£7 10s 11d	20.33%
1767	£71 7s 8d	£3 15s 11d	6.00%
1768	£50 3s 3d	£4 8s 5d	9.33%

TABLE III continued

Year	Total Annual Town Expenditure (N)	Poor Relief Expenditure	Poor Relief Expenditure as % of Total (N)
1769	£126 3s 9d	£3 11s 3d	3.11%
1770	£95 9s 1d	£0 0s 0d	0.00%
1771	£88 6s 8d	£14 14s 2d	17.15%
1772	£78 13s 11d	£5 13s 7d	7.72%
1773	£146 16s	£13 10s 7d	9.40%
1774	£149 12s 9d	£21 12s 4d	14.68%
1775	£114 17s 10d	£29 17s 9d	26.37%
1776	£121 18s 11d	£1 15s	1.84%
1777	£466 19s 7d	£24 2s 3d	5.21%
1778	£1079 8s 3d	£58 1s	5.38%
1779	£9743 1s 2d	£307 15s	3.16%
1780	£54,533 11s	£521 5s	0.96%
1781	£786 9s	£7 5s	0.94%
1782	£960 1s 8d	£38 4d	3.96%
1783	£2068 2s 9d	£32 8s 9d	1.58%
1784	£2133 18s	£44 16s 11d	2.13%
1785	£2170 15s 11d	£48 5s 5d	2.23%

TABLE III continued

Year	Total Annual Town Expenditure (N)	Poor Relief Expenditure	Poor Relief Expenditure as % of Total (N)
1786	£2177 17s 10d	£40 10s 4d	1.85%
1787	£2269 13s 9d	£43 7s 9d	1.92%
1788	£1910 8s 8d	£45 8s 8d	2.39%
1789	£1373 6s 2d	£35 17s 5d	2.64%
1790	£1120 14s 9d	£35 17s 5d	3.25%
1791	£903 14s 11d	£29 8s 10d	3.29%
1792	£933 17s 1d	£25 6d	2.68%
1793	£866 7s 1d	£26 5s 3d	3.05%
1794	£899 1d	£31 16s 8d	3.60%
1795	$1122.27	$19.87	1.77%
1796	$725.13	$286.75	39.54%
1797	$475.22	$138.74	29.19%
1798	$864.22	$44.77	5.18%
1799	$1111.13	$103.81	9.34%
1800	$1048.66	$82.38	7.86%
1801	$727.35	$131.98	18.15%
1802	$627.17	$196.15	31.28%

TABLE III continued

Year	Total Annual Town Expenditure (N)	Poor Relief Expenditure	Poor Relief Expenditure as % of Total (N)
1803	$668.15	$129.59	19.40%
1804	$657.71	$47.75	7.26%
1805	$486.73	$76.42	15.70%
1806	$623.38	$151.12	24.24%
1807	$546.64	$144.95	26.52%
1808	$905.23	$64.10	7.08%
1809	$860.94	$137.76	16.00%
1810	$794.80	$170.21	21.42%
1811	$1325.37	$179.68	13.56%
1812	$1102.13	$242.70	21.92%
1813	$1156.38	$243.67	21.07%
1814	$957.83	$357.66	37.34%
1815	$1051.21	$398.32	37.89%
1816	$1028.33	$177.59	17.27%
1817	$1019.21	$385.90	37.86%
1818	$1021.22	$333.52	32.66%
1819	$1370.23	$487.47	35.57%

TABLE III continued

Year	Total Annual Town Expenditure (N)	Poor Relief Expenditure	Poor Relief Expenditure as % of Total (N)
1820	$1835.19	$259.85	14.16%
1821	$1935.54	$474.73	24.53%
1822	$1200.80	$172.87	14.40%
1823	$1508.31	$151.36	10.04%
1824	$1223.47	$161.12	13.25%
1825	$989.35	$187.22	18.92%
1826	$988.28	$130.59	13.21%
1827	$969.60	$79.34	8.18%
1852	$2011.57	$594.11	29.53%
1854	$2964.42	$653.36	22.04%
1855	$2214.89	$612.34	27.65%
1856		$299.80	
1857		$140.57	
1870	$5875.62	$431.05	7.34%
1880	$3858.65	$103.50	2.68%
1881	$3689.12	$185.05	5.02%
1882	$3426.79	$227.11	6.63%

TABLE III continued

Year	Total Annual Town Expenditure (N)	Poor Relief Expenditure	Poor Relief Expenditure as % of Total (N)
1883	$3419.79	$210.55	6.16%
1884	$3537.34	$280.30	7.92%
1885	$3923.88	$182.00	4.64%
1889	$4189.97	$193.05	4.61%
1890	$3952.54	$302.13	7.64%
1891	$4664.41	$324.24	6.95%

Sources:

Annual Reports (title varies) *1852, 1854-55, 1870, 1880-85, and 1889-91*.

Town Book. Treasurer's Record 1755-1826.

Town of Madbury Expense Account 1856-8.

APPENDIX

Figure 1. The former Lee town poor farm, Wednesday Hill Road, 1982. Presently owned by the LaRoche family, it housed the paupers of Lee from 1837 to 1878.

Poor Relief In Durham, Lee, and Madbury

APPENDIX

Figure 2. The Strafford County poor farm, 1931. Located on County Farm Road in Dover, it was constructed in 1866. Photo courtesy of Margaret W. Ogden, Registrar of Probate, Strafford County Courthouse, Dover.

BIBLIOGRAPHY

ORIGINAL SOURCES

Durham

"Contracts Respecting the Poor of Durham From April 1798," *Records on Paupers and Wharfs, 1798-1806.*

"Disbursements in aid of the families of Volunteers by the Selectmen of Durham prior to March eleventh one thousand eight hundred and sixty-two," *Durham Town Records, Accounts & Business 1700-1866.*

Durham -- Miscellaneous Papers.

Durham, N.H. *Annual Report* (title varies greatly) *1845-47, 1854-56, 1859-70, and 1872-91.*

Durham, N.H. *Copy of the Town Records of the Town of Durham, N.H, 1732-1841,* v. 1-4. (Typed transcripts copied by and under the supervision of Oren V. Henderson, 1942-46).

Durham Town Records, v. 5: *1842-1864.*

Durham Town Records, v. 6: *1865-94.*

Hammond, Isaac W., ed. *Town Papers. Documents Relating to Towns in New Hampshire,* v. XI: *"A" to "F" Inclusive, 1680-1800,* Concord, N.H.: Parsons B. Cogswell, 1882.

Thompson, Benjamin. *Note Book.*

Town of Durham Accounts 1751-1782.

Lee

Hammond, Isaac W., ed. *Town Papers. Documents Relating to Towns in New Hampshire, Gilmanton to New Ipswich*, v. XII: *1647-1800*, Concord, N.H.: Parsons B. Cogswell, 1883.

Lee, N.H. *Annual Report* (title varies) *1844, 1878-79, and 1881-91*.

Lee Town Records 1766-1815. (Copied by Elizabeth L. Stearns, 1901-02).

Memorandum Book for 1784 and 1785.

Miscellaneous Town Papers, 1801-1845.

Payment Book 1809-1825.

Record of Payments and Receipts: Daybook 1802-1809, v. I.

Record of Payments and Receipts: Daybook 1825-1842, v. III.

Town Farm: Yearly Inventory and Appraisal of Property on the Farm 1859-73.

Town Records 1825-1851, 1862-1872, and 1872-1896.

Madbury

Gilman Hall to Selectmen of Madbury, December 30, 1867, Mrs. Forrest C. Twombly, Madbury, N.H.

Madbury, N.H. *Annual Reports* (title varies greatly) *1852-55, 1870, 1880-85, and 1889-91*.

Madbury -- Miscellaneous Town Papers 1768-1799.

Town Book. Treasurer's Record 1755-1826.

Town of Madbury Expense Account 1856-8.

Strafford County

Annual County Commissioners' Report (title varies) *1868-1891*.

New Hampshire. Strafford County. *Register of Deeds*, Books 156, 175, 241, and 264, Dover Court House.

New Hampshire

Batchellor, Albert S., ed. *Laws of New Hampshire*, v. 1 *Province Period 1679-1702*, Manchester, N.H.: John B. Clarke Co., 1904.

Batchellor, Albert S., ed. *Laws of New Hampshire*, v. 2 *Province Period 1702-1745*, Concord, N.H.: Rumford Printing Co., 1913.

Bean, Edwin C., ed. *Laws of New Hampshire*, v. 6-10 *Second Constitutional Period 1792-1801, 1801-1811, 1811-1820, 1821-1828, and 1829-1835*, Concord, N.H.: Evans Printing Co., 1917, 1918, 1920, 1921, and 1922.

Chase, William M. and Arthur H., comp's. and ed's. *The Public Statutes of the State of New Hampshire, and General Laws in Force January 1, 1901*, Concord, N.H.: Edson C. Eastman, 1900.

The Compiled Statutes of the State of New Hampshire: to Which Are Prefixed the Constitutions of the United States and of the State of New Hampshire, Concord, N.H.: G. Parker Lyon, 1853.

Fox, Charles J. *A Guide to Officers of Towns: Containing the Statutes Relating to Their Official Duties, with Forms, Directions and Legal Decisions; Adapted to the Revised Statutes of New Hampshire*, 5th. ed., Samuel C. Eastman, ed. Concord, N.H.: Edson C. Eastman, 1866.

The General Laws of New Hampshire, Manchester, N.H.: John B. Clarke, 1878.

The General Statutes of the State of New Hampshire, Concord, N.H.: B.W. Sanborn & Co., 1867.

Laws of New Hampshire 1853-60, (bound pamphlets).

Laws of the State of New Hampshire; from November Session, 1842, to June Session, 1847, Inclusive, Concord, N.H.: Butterfield & Hill, 1847.

Laws of the State of New Hampshire, Passed January Session, 1891.

Laws of the State of New Hampshire, Passed January Session, 1893 and 1895, Concord, N.H.: Edward N. Pearson, 1893 and 1895.

Laws of the State of New Hampshire, Passed January Session, 1897, 1899, and 1901, Manchester, N.H.: Arthur E. Clarke, 1897, 1899, and 1901.

Laws of the State of New Hampshire, Passed June Session, 1867, Concord, N.H.: B.W. Sanborn Co., 1867.

Laws of the State of New Hampshire, Passed June Session, 1869, Manchester, N.H.: John B. Clarke, 1869.

Laws of the State of New Hampshire, Passed June Session, 1870-1876, Concord, N.H.: B.W. Sanborn & Co., 1870-74, Edward A. Jenks, 1875, and Josiah B. Sanborn, 1876.

Laws of the State of New Hampshire, Passed June Session, 1877, Manchester, N.H.: John B. Clarke, 1877.

Laws of the State of New Hampshire, Passed June Session, 1878-79, and 1883, Concord, N.H.: Josiah B. Sanborn, 1878-79 and Parsons B. Cogswell, 1883.

Laws of the State of New Hampshire, Passed June Session, 1885, 1887, and 1889, Manchester, N.H.: John B. Clarke, 1885, 1887, and 1889.

Metcalf, Henry H., ed. *Laws of New Hampshire*, v. 3 *Province Period 1745-1774* and v. 4 *Revolutionary Period 1776-1784*, Bristol, N.H.: Musgrove Printing House, 1915 and 1916.

Metcalf, Henry H., ed. *Laws of New Hampshire*, v. 5 *First Constitutional Period 1784-1792*, Concord, N.H.: Rumford Press, 1916.

N.H. Laws 1830-39, (bound pamphlets).

The Public Statutes of the State of New Hampshire, Manchester, N.H.: John B. Clarke, 1891.

The Revised Statutes of the State of New Hampshire; Passed December 23, 1842, Concord, N.H.: Carroll & Baker, 1843.

Session Laws of New Hampshire, (bound pamphlets, 1861-66).

SECONDARY SOURCES

Aggregate Amount of Each Description of Persons within the United States of America, and the Territories thereof, Agreeably to Actual Enumeration Made According to Law, in the Year 1810.

Anderson, Leon W. *200 Years of New Hampshire Counties 1771-1971.*

Baier, Ursula, ed. *Lee in Four Centuries,* 1966.

Benton, Josiah H. *Warning Out in New England,* Boston: W. B. Clarke Co., 1911.

Breckinridge, Sophonisba P. *Public Welfare Administration in the United States, Select Documents,* 2nd. ed. Chicago: University of Chicago Press, 1938.

Bremner, Robert H. *American Philanthropy,* Chicago: University of Chicago Press, 1960.

Bremner, Robert H., comp. *American Social History Since 1860,* New York: Appleton-Century-Crofts Educational Division. Meredith Corp., 1971.

Bremner, Robert H., ed. *Children and Youth in America,* v. I: *1600-1865,* Cambridge, Mass.: Harvard University Press, 1970.

Bremner, Robert H. *From the Depths*, New York: New York University Press, 1956.

Coll, Blanche D. *Perspectives in Public Welfare. A History*, Washington: Government Printing Office, 1969.

Commager, Henry S. *The Era of Reform, 1830-1860*, New York: D. Van Nostrand Co., Inc., 1960.

Creech, Margaret. *Three Centuries of Poor Law Administration. A Study of Legislation in Rhode Island*, Chicago: University of Chicago Press, 1936.

DeBow, J.D.B., superintendent of the U.S. Census. *The Seventh Census of the United States: 1850*, Washington: Robert Armstrong, 1853.

DeBow, J.D.B., superintendent of the U.S. Census. *Statistical View of the United States*, Washington: Beverley Tucker, 1854.

Feder, Leah H. *Unemployment Relief in Periods of Depression*, New York: Russell Sage Foundation, 1936.

Fifth Census, or Enumeration of the Inhabitants of the United States in 1830, Washington: Duff Green, 1832.

George, Nellie P. *Old Newmarket New Hampshire*, Exeter, N.H.: News-Letter Press, 1932.

Index to the Laws of New Hampshire, Recorded in the Office of the Secretary of State 1679-1883, Manchester, N.H.: John B. Clarke, 1886.

Jernegan, Marcus W. *Laboring and Dependent Classes in Colonial America 1607-1783*, New York: Frederick Ungar Publishing Co., 1965.

Keller, Morton. *Affairs of State: Public Life in Late Nineteenth Century America*, Cambridge, Mass.: Belknap Press of Harvard University Press, 1977.

Kelso, Robert W. *The History of Public Poor Relief in Massachusetts 1620-1920*, Boston: Houghton Mifflin Co., 1922.

Kennedy, Joseph C.G. *Population of the United States in 1860; Compiled from the Original Returns of the Eighth Census*, Washington: Government Printing Office, 1864.

Knapp, William D. *Somersworth. An Historical Sketch*, 1894.

Leiby, James. *Charity and Corrections in New Jersey*, New Brunswick, N.J.: Rutgers University Press, 1967.

Mencher, Samuel. *Poor Law to Poverty Program*, Pittsburgh: University of Pittsburgh Press, 1967.

Mennel, Robert and Spackman, Steven. "Origins of Welfare in the States: Albert G. Byers and the Ohio Board of State Charities," (unpublished paper).

Morison, Elizabeth F. and Elting E. *New Hampshire. A Bicentennial History*, New York: W.W. Norton & Co., Inc., 1976.

McDuffee, Franklin. *History of the Town of Rochester, New Hampshire, From 1722 to 1890*, v. II. Manchester, N.H.: John B. Clarke, 1892.

Nash, Gary B. *The Urban Crucible*, Cambridge, Mass.: Harvard University Press, 1979.

The New Hampshire Historical Records Survey Project Division of Professional and Service Projects. Works Projects Administration. (Sponsored by U.N.H.). *Town Government in New Hampshire*, Manchester, N.H.: N.H. Historical Records Survey Project, 1940.

Nye, A.E.G., comp. *Dover, N.H., Its History and Industries Issued as an Illustrated Souvenir in Commemoration of the Twenty-fifth Anniversary of Foster's Daily Democrat*, Dover, N.H.: George J. Foster & Co., 1898.

Porter, Robert P., superintendent. *Compendium of the Eleventh Census: 1890, Part I -- Population*, Washington: Government Printing Office, 1892.

Return of the Whole Number of Persons Within the Several Districts of the United States, According to "An Act Providing for the Enumeration of the Inhabitants of the United States," Passed March the First, One Thousand

Seven Hundred and Ninety-One, Philadelphia: Childs and Swaine, 1791.

Return of the Whole Number of Persons Within the Several Districts of the United States, According to "An Act Providing for the Second Census or Enumeration of the Inhabitants of the United States", Washington: Duane Printer, 1801.

Rothman, David J. *The Discovery of the Asylum*, Boston: Little, Brown, and Co., 1971.

Rush, John A. *The City-County Consolidated*, Los Angeles: John A. Rush, 1942.

Sanborn, Frank B. *New Hampshire. An Epitome of Popular Government*, Boston: Houghton, Mifflin and Co., 1904.

Scales, John. *History of Strafford County New Hampshire and Representative Citizens*, Chicago: Richmond-Arnold Publishing Co., 1914.

Sixth Census or Enumeration of the Inhabitants of the United States, as Corrected at the Department of State, 1840, Washington: Blair and Rives, 1841.

Statistics of the Population of the United States at the Tenth Census (June 1, 1880), Washington: Government Printing Office, 1883.

Swindler, William F. and Vexler, Robert I., ed's. *Chronological and Documentary Handbook of the State of New Hampshire*, Dobbs Ferry, N.Y.: Oceana Publications, 1978.

Tyler, Alice F. *Freedom's Ferment*, Freeport, N.Y.: Books for Libraries Press, 1970.

Walker, Francis A. *A Compendium of the Ninth Census (June 1, 1870) Compiled Pursuant to a Concurrent Resolution of Congress, and Under the Direction of the Secretary of the Interior*, Washington: Government Printing Office, 1872.

Walker, Francis A., superintendent of the census. *Ninth Census*, v. I *The Statistics of the Population of the United States*, Washington:

Government Printing Office, 1872.

Weeden, William B. *Economic and Social History of New England 1620-1789*, Boston: Houghton, Mifflin, and Co., 1891.

Wines, Frederick H. *Report on Crime, Pauperism, and Benevolence in the United States at the Eleventh Census: 1890. Part II General Tables*, Washington: Government Printing Office, 1895.

Wines, Frederick H. *Report on the Defective, Dependent, and Delinquent Classes of the Population of the United States, As Returned at the Tenth Census (June 1, 1880)*, Washington: Government Printing Office, 1888.

ARTICLES

Almy, Frederic. "Public or Private Outdoor Relief." *Proceedings of the National Conference of Charities and Correction at the Twenty-Seventh Annual Session Held in the City of Topeka, Kan., May 18-24, 1900*, (1901), pp. 134-145.

Berthoff, Rowland. "Reviews of Books. Americas." *American Historical Review*, 77 (April 1972), pp. 585-586.

Bicknell, Ernest. "Observations on Official Outdoor Poor Relief." *Proceedings...at the Twenty-Fourth Annual Session Held in Toronto, Ontario, July 7-14, 1897*, (1898), pp. 249-256.

Blackmar, F.W. "Social Degeneration in Towns and Rural Districts." *Proceedings...1900*, (1901), pp. 115-124.

Blodgett, I.N. "New Hampshire." *Proceedings...1897*, (1898), pp. 415-416.

Blodgett, I.N. "Reports from States. New Hampshire." *Proceedings...at* the *Twenty-Fifth Annual Session Held in the City of New York, May 18-25, 1898*, (1899), pp. 69-70.

Blodgett, I.N. "Reports from States. New Hampshire." *Proceedings...at the Twenty-Eighth Annual Session Held in the City of Washington, D.C., May 9-15, 1901*, (1901), pp. 78-79.

Brackett, Jeffrey R. "Public Outdoor Relief in the United States." *Proceedings...at the Forty-Second Annual Session Held in the City of Baltimore, Md., May 12-19, 1915*, (1915), pp. 446-458.

Butler, Amos W. "Official Outdoor Relief and the State." *Proceedings...1915*, (1915), pp. 437-445.

Butler, Amos W. "Saving the Children." *Proceedings...1901*, (1901), pp. 204-218.

Buzelle, George B. "Report of the Committee." *Proceedings...at the Nineteenth Annual Session Held in the City of Denver, Col., June 23-29, 1892*, (1892), pp. 204-211.

Byers, Albert G. "Boards of State Charities." *Proceedings...at the Sixteenth Annual Session Held in San Francisco, Cal., September 11-18, 1889*, (1889), pp. 99-102.

Clark, A.W. "Limits to State Control and Supervision." *Proceedings...at the Thirty-First Annual Session Held in the City of Portland, Me., June 15-22, 1904*, pp. 180-187.

Clark, Mary V. "The Almshouse." *Proceedings...1900*, (1901), pp. 146-158.

Coben, Stanley. "The United States of America." *Collier's Encyclopedia*, v. 22 (1977), pp. 666A-743.

Curti, Merle. "American Philanthropy and the National Character." *American Quarterly*, 10 (1958), pp. 420-437.

Daniels, George H. "Book Reviews." *Journal of American History*, 58 (March 1972), pp. 1015-1017.

Deutsch, Albert. "The Sick Poor in Colonial Times." *American Historical Review*, 46 (1941), pp. 560-579.

Folks, Homer. "The Removal of Children from Almshouses." *Proceedings...at the Twenty-First Annual Session Held in the City of Nashville, Tenn., May 23-29, 1894*, (1894), pp. 119-132.

Gavisk, Francis. "State Supervision. Report of the Committee." *Proceedings...at the Thirty-Eighth Annual Session Held in the City of Boston, Mass., June 7-14, 1911*, (1911), pp. 9-12.

Gillette, Arthur J. "The State Care of Indigent, Crippled, and Deformed Children." *Proceedings...1904*, pp. 285-294.

Hart, H. Hastings. "Report of the Committee on Reports from States." *Proceedings...1897*, (1898), pp. 362-374.

Hart, H. Hastings. "Report of the Committee on State Boards of Charities." *Proceedings...1889*, (1889), pp. 89-99.

Henderson, Charles R. *et al.* "Politics in Charitable and Penal Institutions. Report of the Committee." *Proceedings...1898*, (1899), pp. 237-246.

Henderson, Charles R. "Poor Laws of the United States." *Proceedings...1897*, (1898), pp. 256-271.

Hoffman, Frederick L. "Statistics of Poverty and Pauperism." *Proceedings...at the Thirty-Fourth Annual Session Held in the City of Minneapolis, Minn., June 12th. to 19th., 1907*, (1907), pp. 132-154.

Hubbard, C.M. "The Relation of Intemperance to Dependency." *Proceedings...1907*, (1907), pp. 335-362.

Kelley, Florence. "Child Labor Laws." *Proceedings...1904*, pp. 268-273.

Klebaner, Benjamin J. "Pauper Auctions: The 'New England Method' of Poor Relief." *Essex Institute Historical Collections*, 91 (1955), pp. 195-210.

Letchworth, William P. "The Removal of Children from Almshouses in the State of New York." *Proceedings...1894*, (1894), pp. 132-136.

McCulloch, Oscar C. "Report of the Standing Committee." *Proceedings...1889*, (1889), pp. 10-24.

Mullenbach, James. "The Sifting Process and the Unemployed." *Proceedings...at the Forty-Third Annual Session Held in the City of Indianapolis, Ind., May 10-17, 1916*, (1916), pp. 191-199.

"Report of the Committee. History of State Boards." *Proceedings...at the Twentieth Annual Session Held in the City of Chicago, Ill., June 8-11, 1893*, (1893), pp. 33-52.

"Report of the Committee on Reports from States. New Hampshire." *Proceedings...1889*, (1889), pp. 152-156.

"Reports from States. New Hampshire." *Proceedings...1894*, (1894), p. 250.

Rosengarten, Joseph G. "A Successful Experiment in Utilizing Unemployed Labor." *Proceedings...1894*, (1894), pp. 58-62.

Rosenkrantz, Barbara G. "Booby-Hatch or Booby Trap: A New Look at Nineteenth Century Reform." *Social Research*, 39 (Winter 1972), pp. 733-743.

Shurtleff, H.S. "State Care of Destitute Infants -- The Massachusetts System." *Proceedings...1889*, (1889), pp. 1-5.

Streeter, Mrs. Frank S. "Reports from States. New Hampshire." *Proceedings...1904*, pp. 71-76.

Streeter, Mrs. Frank S. "Reports from States. New Hampshire." *Proceedings...1907*, (1907), pp. 558-559.

Trusdell, C.G. "The History of Public and Private Indoor and Outdoor Relief." *Proceedings...1893*, (1893), pp. 94-105.

White, William J. "State Supervision of Private Charitable Institutions." *Proceedings...1907*, (1907), pp. 78-85.

Wright, A.O. "Employment in Poorhouses." *Proceedings...1889*, (1889), pp. 197-203.

Wright, A.O. "Report of the Committee on History of Reports from States." *Proceedings...1893*, (1893), pp. 57-58.

Wyllie, Irvin G. "The Search for an American Law of Charity, 1776-1844." *Mississippi Valley Historical Review*, 46 (1959), pp. 203-221.

www.ingramcontent.com/pod-product-compliance
Lightning Source LLC
Chambersburg PA
CBHW070454090426
42735CB00012B/2544